AIRSTREAM LIVING

AIRSTREAM *Living*

BRUCE LITTLEFIELD AND SIMON BROWN

HARPER
DESIGN

An Imprint of HarperCollinsPublishers

First published in 2005 by:
Harper Design
An Imprint of HarperCollins*Publishers*
195 Broadway, New York, NY 10007
Tel: (212) 207-7000
Fax: 855-746-6023
harperdesign@harpercollins.com
www.hc.com

This book was conceived, designed, and produced by
Ivy Press

210 High Street, Lewes, East Sussex BN7 2NS, UK
Creative Director PETER BRIDGEWATER
Publisher SOPHIE COLLINS
Publisher, Lifestyle JUDITH MORE
Editorial Director JASON HOOK
Art Director KARL SHANAHAN
Senior Project Editor CAROLINE EARLE
Designer BERNARD HIGTON
Picture Research ANNA DAVIES, KELLY GRIFFIN

Distributed throughout North America by:
HarperCollins*Publishers*
195 Broadway
New York, NY 10007

Library of Congress Control Number: 2005926116
ISBN: 978-0-06-115164-4

Contents

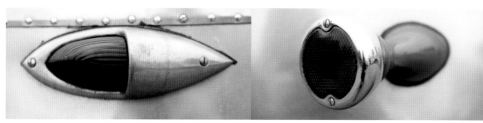

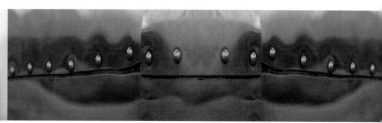

INTRODUCTION

This is the riveting tale of those who have "aluminum fever" and the trailers that gave it to them. Though the symptoms are not the same, nor are the ages or types of people who get it, the diagnosis is—it's incurable. The only treatment is to get into it and have fun.

Since the early 1920s, we've been "recreating" in vehicles. From backyard to freeway, from city to country, from retro to futuristic, silver trailers have played an important role in our holidays, escapes, and retreats, and have become an icon of American design.

And it's not just about the name. Though Airstream is a brand name and a legend, there are literally hundreds of types of silver trailers, from homemade contraptions to assembly-line beauties such as Crown, El Rey, and Spartan.

No, there's something else about these uniquities. We fancy them for reasons as inimitable and individual as we are. It's the way they make us feel, the playfulness they bring out, the fantasy they reflect. So, a warning before you turn another page: *silver fever is contagious.* Once you've caught it, you'll always dream in silver.…

There was an Airstream behind the Simmons's house when I was growing up. It was the most unique thing about my small-town South Carolina neighborhood—sleek, shiny, and silver—and anytime I had friends over, I'd take the opportunity to show off the "spaceship" that had landed in the Simmons's backyard.

Every Friday night of the summer, Mr. and Mrs. Simmons would pack their yippy toy poodle, Precious, a couple bags of groceries from the Piggly Wiggly and two aluminum lounge chairs into their wood-paneled Ford station wagon, and tow the silver ship to a campground at Lake Murray. With all the preparation for and hoopla surrounding their weekly departure, you'd have thought they were pioneers leaving for the unknown. But Lake Murray was only 3½ miles away. Every Sunday afternoon, as sure as church, the trio (Mr. Simmons, the Mrs., and Precious) would drive back down Hill Springs Drive after a weekend of fun at the lake, and then we children would stop mid-chase to greet their luminous return. Mrs. Simmons would wave to us and their Airstream followed suit—reflecting a dozen or so waving arms and the admiring faces of its young fans, standing in front of our cookie-cutter brick houses.

Mr. Simmons didn't acknowledge us. His attention was always on the mathematical angle he had calculated to position his Ford so that he could back his huge land yacht (fresh from its Lake Murray adventure) up their driveway and into the backyard. He would drive a little ways past his mailbox toward the cul-de-sac on an angle and then slip the Ford into reverse, maneuvering their weekend house strategically up the driveway, through the gates of their chain-link fence, and into its workweek spot in their backyard. I'm not sure what they did while they were at Lake Murray, but my young mind's fantasy was that they were meeting with other space travelers and planning the time they were all going back into space.

The summer after Mr. Simmons died of a heart attack, David Ruff and I decided, in a moment of fourth-grade mischief, to sneak inside the Airstream and check it out. I was amazed by the tiny tub, the toilet, the spacious bed, and then, while I examined the interior of the miniature refrigerator, David squealed from the sofa, "MRS. SIMMONS!" I clunked my head on the top of the refrigerator and stumbled backwards. "HIDE!" we both yelped, like two burglars caught red-handed. I'm sure what Mrs. Simmons saw was a trailer rocking like a storm-tossed boat, as both David and I scurried about attempting to find the perfect spot to take cover. One thing I learned that day is that just about every square inch of an Airstream is used for something. There just aren't a lot of hiding spots!

Mrs. Simmons found me in the tiny tub, covered beneath a couple of terrycloth towels, and David was easily spotted as the awkward lump behind the plaid sofa cushions. Fortunately, Mrs. Simmons smiled kindly upon us that day—perhaps realizing someone should enjoy her Airstream. She told us we could make her Airstream our "clubhouse" that summer, as long as we took care of it and washed it for her "a couple of times."

Oh, the summer of 1978. David and I must have washed and polished Mrs. Simmons's Airstream 30 times, but…I learned how to play poker (Mrs. Simmons taught David and me around the flip-up Formica-topped table); we ate a lot of Kraft Macaroni & Cheese (Mrs. Simmons thought she was Julia Child in the galley kitchen), and I kissed Paula Shull during a virginal game of spin the bottle. (Mrs. Simmons had Garden Club on Thursday nights!)

The next summer, Mrs. Simmons sold her house and loaded up the Ford. She, Precious, and our silver clubhouse moved to live near her daughter in Hollywood, Florida, and Paula Shull dumped me for Pate Cox. And, as I discovered, an Airstream is a lot like a first love: you are lured by her charm, seduced by her beauty, and once bitten, you are forever chasing after her mystique.

In an Airstream, your home away from home is where you stop.

There are countless stories of why and how and what and who made Airstream owners become Airstream owners, and what and how and why they do what they do with them once they have them. And that is the story of this book. Little did I know in 1979—as Mrs. Simmons and her Airstream made their last trip past my house—that 25 years later I'd be writing a book about one of the most recognizable pieces of Americana. Or that I would almost own an Airstream of my very own....

WALLY BYAM

According to legend, Wally Byam's story started quite simply: his wife refused to go camping without a kitchen. And Wally loved to camp. So, in the late 1920s, Wally created a travel trailer that had a kitchen. And he and Stella went camping. Not satisfied with the "crude, boxy structure which rested none too easily upon a Model A Ford chassis," Wally began making improvements and alterations in his camper, including dropping the floor below the axles to provide headroom and using lighter-weight materials. Despite the stock market crash of 1929, Wally threw caution to the wind and abandoned his law, advertising, and publishing careers to begin marketing a do-it-yourself trailer kit. The public liked his trailers so much that he began custom-building them in his Los Angeles backyard, while supplementing his income as a salesman for trailer designer William Hawley Bowlus, a former pilot and ace glider designer.

By 1935, by which time Bowlus had introduced the strong-as-steel alloy, "Duraluminum," in his design, the Bowlus trailers were priced too expensively for what the depressed market could bear and his company rolled into bankruptcy. Wally bought the company at auction and, in 1936, introduced the official Airstream Clipper, so named because Wally thought it moved down the road like a

"stream of air." (That and it was the spitting image of the aerodynamic Pan Am Clipper, minus the wings!) The riveted "monocoque" body housed a galley, a dinette booth that converted into a bed, a water supply, electric lights, and a dry ice air-conditioning unit that could keep four occupants cool. By dumping the traditional canned-ham-as-travel-trailer shape in favor of the aerodynamic Clipper, Wally Byam had created a legend.

The sleek Airstream trailer has grown up to become an international design icon. In fact, *Money* magazine named the Airstream one of the "99 Things That, Yes, Americans Make Best," putting Airstream in the company of such American stalwarts as Campbell's Soup, Levi's Jeans, and Crayola Crayons. Yes, the Airstream is instantly recognizable—a brand name that has so overshadowed its competition it not only denotes itself, but has become a generic classification. Much like Kleenex, Q-Tips, and Jello have come to be all tissues, swabs, and wobbly gelatin products, so has the name Airstream come to represent all things silvery and trailerlike. Though thousands of different trailer models have traveled the highways, only one is the namesake. To the uninitiated, Airstream can indicate any silver trailer, but to the purist, only an Airstream is an Airstream, and everything else is like, well, just an ordinary box of gelatin.

"All the travel fun you ever dreamed about" promised Wally Byam (right) about his distinctive, aerodynamic, aluminum-shelled trailer. What Wally was selling more than a trailer was an experience—the experience of the open road, of meeting people, of seeing the world. In short, Wally was selling freedom. And 75 years later, the Airstream allure is attracting an ever-growing set of freedom seekers eager to script their own experience.

OTHER MAKES

If it walks like a duck and quacks like a duck, it must be a duck, right? Not exactly, especially when we're talking silver trailers.

Just because it is silver doesn't mean it's an Airstream. In fact, in 1936 there were over 300 trailer companies manufacturing a wide variety of travel trailers, and even though only one survived, that leaves a lot of other mystery vintage trailers floating around with names as assorted as their structure: Avion, Spartan, Silver Streak, Cayo, Alma, Fan, Yellowstone, and Prairie Schooner are just a few.

And there were other people in the silver rush besides Wally Byam, leading their companies to financial success. People like the enterprising J. P. Getty who, like Wally, recognized the need for affordable yet quality housing in the post-World War II era. He took his experience helming the fabrication of such craft as the Navy NP1 trainer and components for the B24 bombers for Spartan's war effort and put it into trailers. His trailers, such as the Spartan Manor, were similar to the look of Airstreams, but Spartan's larger models, though "mobile," were most often "park models" and used as permanent housing because of their immense size. The Mansion and Royal Mansion, for example, were both 33 feet long—not what you might take up to Mt. Rushmore for the weekend.

What is sometimes called Airstream's sister, the Silver Streak, looks so similar to an Airstream that people are often fooled

Flxible (left), originally a motorcycle sidecar company, began manufacturing team buses and motor homes when Ford cars began to quash the sidecar business. The Silver Streak (above) is so similar in appearance to the name brand, it is sometimes known as Airstream's sister. The Spartan Company (right) produced "park models," or mobile homes, that were made with permanent residence in mind. All of them, like Airstream, provide a welcome mat to silver living.

(I was!). The reason is that Curtis Wright started a manufacturing plant in Los Angeles shortly before World War II and hired a man named Wally Byam, whose Airstream company was on hold because structural aluminum was classified as critical war material, available only for the building of vital aircraft. Wally used his skills with Duraluminum to assist Curtis's company in war production, and shortly after the war ended, the twosome started production of a travel trailer based on Wally's prewar Airstream Clipper and Silver Cloud models at the Van Nuys Airport. When a disagreement between the two occurred, they went their separate ways—Wally back to generating Airstreams and Curtis on to producing Curtis Wright Travel Trailers. In June of 1949, Curtis sold the business and the new owners began producing trailers under the Silver Streak name in El Monte, California, and continued until the 1970s.

Just as with fine wine and spicy food, it is all a matter of taste. Some people, who like to be the "outsider," love the rare creatures whose parts are ever so hard to come by. They love the thrill of the hunt, of having something that's different from the pack. And others wouldn't have anything but the original. Either way—Coke or Pepsi, vodka or gin, toe-may-toe or toe-mah-toe—the only thing that really matters is that it's yours and it's silver.

290

Flxible

SPARTANETTE

TANDEM

29564

AIRSTREAM

International

ANOTHER QUALITY PRODUCT · THE WORLD OF AIRSTREAM

A

UL·8619

NY EMPIRE STATE 60

NEW YORK

84718W

TRAILER

Bambi

TAKE IT EASY

AIRSTREAM

4030

12804 E. FIRESTONE BLVD.
NORWALK, CALIFORNIA

NATIVE
Denver Trailer Sales
Greater DENVER, CO.

The Caravan Club, a club in which trailers, not their owners, are registered members, is still actively organizing caravans throughout the world, and continues to abide by the one-trailer-one-vote system, which keeps the club democratic and encourages its participants to help each other out. Caravanners in 1959 spent their final days on the Cape Town to Cairo trip at the Great Pyramid in Giza, Egypt, lined up in the "wagon-wheel" formation, Wally's way of giving all participants a feeling of equality and community.

ON THE ROAD

Airstreams hit the mainstream in the 1950s, when Wally began leading excursions through the Wally Byam Caravan Club International (WBCCI). "Adventure is where you find it," Wally proclaimed. "Any place, every place, except at home in a rocking chair." And Americans, enamored with the idea of owning their own home, were especially delighted that they could own a home and travel in it to see America, and then beyond. Wally's blue-bereted caravanners followed him all over the world—from Central America to Europe, from India to Egypt. Buying an Airstream became and remains a ticket into a private party. At 10,000 members strong, the WBCCI is the world's oldest recreational vehicle club, holding nearly 1,500 rallies annually.

Wally wanted to expunge people's fears of travel by promising all the creature comforts of home at a price everyone could afford. His ads promised functional, efficient, and safe living that would allow families (read: your wife will love it!) an opportunity to discover America without breaking the bank.

During the glory days of travel, families would pack their bags and their cameras and journey out in their trailers to discover America—from sea to shining sea. What they found was that their trailers would often attract as much attention as the destinations.

NO CHANGES, ONLY IMPROVEMENTS

Perhaps the reason that Airstream is the only one of the 300 post-Depression era trailer companies to survive is that Wally adopted a simple strategy: "Let's not make changes, let's only make improvements." Or perhaps, on an emotional level, it's because of the Airstream experience that Wally made possible.

The Airstream body style has undergone only five "improvements" since the original Clipper. Designers learned that to stray from Wally's winning formula was a surefire road to disaster. Twenty-five years after Wally's death, engineers decided it was time for a change, and the "Land Yacht" (R.I.P. 1989–1991) found its life cut shorter than its squared-off front. The short-lived beige box died an untimely death when Airstream enthusiasts dubbed it the "Squarestream." The Land Yacht joined "New Coke" as a gigantic blunder and served as a reminder to tinkerers: don't mess with success. Like Coke, the Airstream exterior is a timeless American classic.

Fortunately, however, even the purists haven't remained wed

At $1,200, the first Clipper (top left) was considered expensive, especially during the Depression years. Today's highway behemoths, like the Land Yacht XL (left) and the SkyDeck, will run upwards of $250,000, but are highly sophisticated with many modern conveniences. Some, suitable for rock stars and heads of state, are rolling palaces, retrofitted with lush fixtures such as gold-plated knobs, marble floors, buttery leathers, and inlaid cabinetry.

Fortunately, however, even the purists haven't remained wed to the Airstream's interior. The aged beige vinyl panels and the cream-colored carpets have been allowed to change with time, without much argument.

In 2000, San Francisco-based architect and furniture designer Christopher Deam was commissioned by New York-based design firm Inside Design to rethink a trade show booth for plastic laminate manufacturer Wilsonart to premiere at the International Contemporary Furniture Fair. Deam's mission was to use the manufacturer's laminate surfaces to redecorate a vintage 1948 Airstream Wanderer. Deam worked day and night for seven weeks stripping away everything that wasn't absolutely essential within the Wanderer's interior, hoping to lessen the disconnect between the inside and the outside of the trailer. What he uncovered was a hidden masterpiece.

When Deam peeled back the dated suburban paneling and took the innards down to the shiny interior aluminum, the trailer felt bigger and brighter, and by using cool ice-blue and gray laminates

If your plans include extended cross-country trips (and your budget is equally extended), perhaps the luxury of a motor home is right for you. They're roomy, and include amenities like a residential-style bathroom, a dining "room," and lights, water, and refrigeration that are all independent of outside resources. And let's be honest, if you can afford to buy it, you're not worried about the gas mileage.

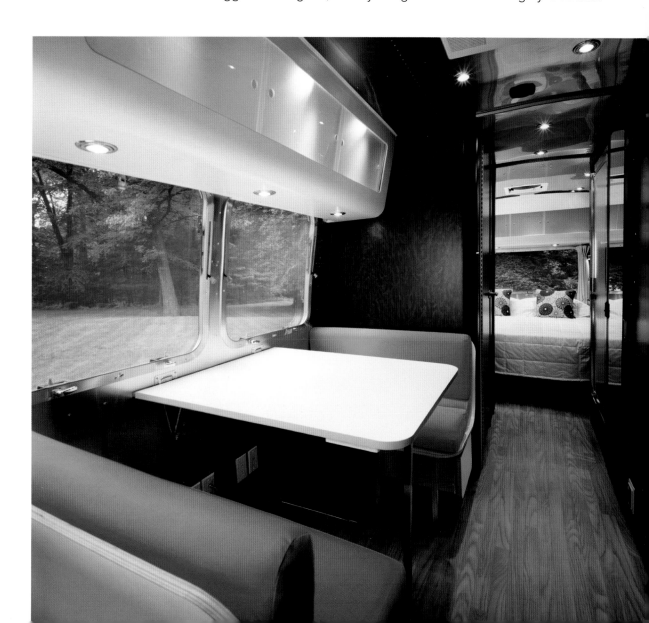

he created aesthetically pleasing interior surfaces. He also added backlit, translucent Plexiglas sliding doors, Internet workstations, sound systems, glass-top stoves, and stainless-steel sinks. Then, by removing all the plastic trim and rubber window frames from the exterior, he made the outside exclusively aluminum, leaving nothing to distract the eye from the hand-riveted shiny shell. The result? Deam's redo made the 1948 Wanderer familiar but futuristic, spacious, and modern, with an inside that was as pleasing as the outside. Even Airstream diehards bit.

The new look, christened the "Crossroads," created quite the buzz at the fair and reinvigorated design interest in Airstream, especially from the executives at Thor Industries, the parent company of Airstream. After the fair, Thor contracted Inside Design and Deam to conceive a 16-foot Bambi model, and what was born ain't your grandpa's Airstream.

The International CCD model (hint: Christopher C. Deam) went on the market at the beginning of 2002 and quickly became Airstream's best seller. There are now five CCD models, which are attracting a new set of young fans as well as pleasing traditional devotees. The older crowd suggests it gives them fond reminiscences of 1950s diners, while the younger crowd drools over its Jetson's high-tech chic. The CCD has been exhibited in the San Francisco Museum of Modern Art, and *Fortune* magazine named it one of the "25 Best Products of the Year," suggesting that the result has struck the perfect balance between respect for what made Airstream an icon and modern contemporary design.

About 550 trailers roll out of the company's headquarters at Jackson Center, Ohio, each year. To date, more than 115,000 Airstreams have been built, and of those, an estimated 80,000 are still on the road. New Airstreams range from around $30,000 for a 16-foot Bambi to $85,000 for a decked-out Limited (complete with fireplace!). Unrestored vintage prices can range from "just get it off my property," to $5,000, to "make me an offer I can't refuse," depending on size, age, and the sentimentality or greediness of those in possession. Whether used as an alternative to motels or as yard sculpture, Airstreams have become a distinct part of the American (and now international) landscape.

Next on the horizon for Airstream is a joint venture with auto company Nissan. Airstream wanted to produce a smaller, lighter model that could be towed by a typical passenger car, and Nissan designed the answer. Its Base Camp, a small (15-foot) trailer with integrated Kelty tent, is receiving rave reviews from enthusiasts and should hit the market in early 2006 at a price below $20,000. It will have a versatile interior space that can serve as both living quarters and also as a "toy box" for outdoor gear.

Even though Airstream is an icon of design, the company's management team is eager to enhance and widen the brand's appeal. The interior of this Bambi was specially designed by Quiksilver as a pool house for Airstream President Dicky Riegel.

Nissan designers borrowed three Airstreams while renovations were taking place at Nissan headquarters and the result was a new trailer concept. The Nissan Base Camp, targeted at the adventurous set, can be towed by a typical passenger car.

LIVE MORE, SEE MORE, DO MORE

If the enthusiasm for Airstreams has always been contagious, we're now in the middle of an epidemic. As we hit the seventy-fifth anniversary of Wally's answer to his wife's camping-without-a-kitchen dilemma, Airstreams and their cousins have become "in" with everyone from the style-savvy to the surfer-boy-next-door. There's a rolling-real-estate land rush on, and it seems that everyone wants to own a gleaming aluminum chunk.

The trailers have been featured in movies (*Charlie's Angels*), album covers (Sheryl Crow), and commercials (Mountain Dew). MTV installed a 1957 model as its waiting room for its West Coast headquarters. Celebrities Tom Hanks, David Duchovny, Anthony Edwards, and Sean Penn are all Airstream owners. Paris and Nicole drove cross-country in one. And director Tim Burton recently bought his third. There's an Airstream line of furniture, Airstream diner, Airstream guitar, and a Hotwheels Airstream miniature. Neiman Marcus has even marketed a custom-designed Airstream bedecked in luxurious fabrics, inlaid wood paneling, antique rugs and hand-painted murals worthy of the Sistine Chapel. The cost? A mere $195,000 (delivery not included).

Yes, even though it never left, the Airstream is back. And everywhere they go—no matter the size, age, or style—their shiny shell attracts attention and sets dreamers to dreaming. Wally and his Airstream continue "to strive endlessly to stir the venturesome spirit that moves you to follow a rainbow to its end." They've become movie star dressing rooms, mobile offices, pool houses, art studios, hotdog stands, guest cottages, galleries, bars, and anything else that the imagination can dream up. Tourists use them as photo ops; truckers honk; children wave. And they reflect what we need them to be.

Airstreams don't discriminate. Titleholders cross class, age, professions, and country lines. All an Airstream requires is a sense of adventure. As I've talked with hundreds of Airstream owners, designers, and dreamers, I've gotten the sense that Airstreams are purchased with the heart much more than the head. Like a smitten

Today's Airstream advertising reminds us that there are "52 Weekends" in a year, but now that there's so much more we do in our Airstreams, we can't be limited to just weekends. From families to astronauts to designers, they've become a piece of Americana we won't live without, but we'll find a thousand ways to live within.

schoolboy, Airstreamers are so infatuated that they look past details like capacities and tow load. All they know (or want to know) is how it makes them feel. Yep, much like a first love. Or maybe it runs even deeper. Maybe the Airstream is like the womb—cozy, comfortable, and able to adapt to suit our needs. Sort of a womb with a view.

Wally was right: when you own a piece of rolling real estate, "home is where you stop." So, where does your imagination take you? How do you want to live life in your silver palace? What follows are a few ideas....

Welcome to Airstream Living.

Part One
LIFE IN A LAND YACHT

Travel trailer owners can no longer be squeezed into one of two traditional molds—"vacationer" or "retired couple." The molds have been broken and life in a land yacht has taken on infinite possibilities. From poolside cabana to teen party space to backyard dance hall, these silver beauties have made the word "trailer" chic.

Those unique aerodynamic curves and silver shells have been attracting fans like bees to honey for years, but now those fans cross a wide demographic spectrum—young and old, rich and poor, famous and not—and have cut a wide design swath as colorful as a wall of paint chips in a hardware store. The interiors range from museum-quality vintage preservations to safari-themed gut conversions.

The only thing certain about the land yacht is that whatever the style, people will always want to sneak a peek in your windows. They're not trying to catch you in your undies, they're just interested in what you've done with the place. So, put out the welcome mat. As Wally Byam once said, "When you travel in a trailer, you meet people in their homes and they meet you in theirs." Welcome home....

Wheel and Testament

Owner: Laura Woodroffe
Location: Bath, England
Model: Bambi II Airstream

When Laura Woodroffe first visited her godmother's Airstream Bambi, she fell in love with it. Being only 11 years old at the time, she had never seen anything so enchanting. To her it was the ideal clubhouse and the perfect place to have a tea party with her beloved godmother. Little did she know then that less than a year later it would be hers.

Antiques dealer Lynda Trahair bought her Bambi II Airstream from a couple named Dave and Jenny and, according to the leather-bound diary found in her Airstream when she passed away, the day they dropped it off Lynda felt terrified. "Suddenly, I'm in possession of this vehicle with all its technical bits," she wrote. "A bit like arriving home with a first baby after having a nice safe hospital with all those expert nurses to call on. It looks very alien, but also quite pretty, especially in the moonlight when it glows distinctly."

Within days, she was discovering new tricks within the silver beauty (like the chopping board beneath the sink cover) and welcoming friends like goddaughter Laura and her parents, Lucy, Lynda's best friend, and her husband, Patrick, a lighting designer. It was the first time they'd seen an Airstream, and as they sat inside looking out at the beautiful, sunny valley, Pat asked, "Why is it more fun sitting inside than outside?"

Laura Woodroffe loves to invite her friends from the Radford Farm School into her backyard for parties in her Bambi, left to her in the codicil of her godmother's will. Each June, she and her family take the Bambi on a road trip to the Glastonbury Music Festival, where they camp and enjoy the largest greenfield music and performing arts festival in the world.

The interior of Laura Woodroffe's Airstream was thoughtfully designed by her godmother. She weighed every decision, from choosing deck-chair stripe over "kitsch zebra" to blue-and-cream versus silver-leaf walls.

Lynda began to baby her Bambi, cleaning the interior crevices with a toothbrush and measuring for blinds to replace "the horrid, naff curtains." She draped the interior with samples of fabrics, debating the pros and cons of a classy blue-and-cream deck-chair stripe or a kitsch zebra stripe, and asked opinions of passersby who often stopped to ask questions and coo over her new arrival.

When her husband Nidge left town on business, she decided to camp out in the Airstream with "a banana, an apple, a spot of green tea, and a newspaper." She wondered what she would do if prowlers disturbed her, as a neighbor "who thinks in tabloid newspaper terms" had feared, but fell asleep beneath the twinkling stars of the skylight like a comforted fetus enveloped in a silver womb.

During the time spent with her Airstream, Lynda made a lot of discoveries about the clever gadgets within it, and made a profound observation about the nature of people by how they responded to the Airstream. There were, she determined, two kinds of people: those who looked mystified at her delight in it and those who, like children, were bright-eyed and eager to revel in adventure. Perhaps that's why when she fell ill that summer with pancreatic cancer, she got out her will and wrote in a codicil bequeathing her Airstream to Laura, her 11-year-old goddaughter, whose parents also shared Lynda's childlike joy for life. She knew that it would continue to be well used and well loved.

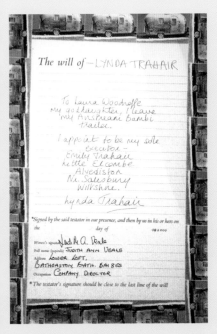

Antiques dealer Lynda Trahair loved
her Bambi so much that she would
regularly clean it with a toothbrush.
She made sure that she bequeathed
it to someone who would cherish
it in the same way. Today, it is
nestled in the beautiful English
countryside, near Bath.

Backyard Star

Owner: Aidan and Elizabeth Quinn
Location: Ulster County, New York
Model: 1961 Airstream Bambi

When you think of a celebrity's backyard you might conjure up images of an ornately tiled swimming pool or a Ferrari parked in front of extensive gardens, not a 1961 Airstream Bambi turned dance hall/craft services wagon. But then actors husband and wife Aidan Quinn and Elizabeth Bracco aren't your typical celebrities—they maintain a real life outside of their reel life.

Perhaps the secret to their successful 18-year marriage comes from their willingness to be spontaneous and their sense of fun. Take, for example, the way they acquired their Airstream. They'd admired it for awhile from a distance, driving each weekend back and forth down a country road where it was parked. One day, like giggling trick or treaters, the couple went up to the house, knocked on the door, and asked if it was for sale.

Elizabeth Bracco Quinn says the Airstream is "the greatest sculpture ever made." After drumming up the courage to knock on the door of a house where it sat in a neighboring town, they bought the Bambi for $4,000 from a couple who'd owned it for 40 years.

One of the happiest and most romantic couples in Hollywood doesn't live in Hollywood at all. Aidan and Elizabeth Quinn spend their life far away from Los Angeles in the Catskill region of New York, where Lizzie often throws backyard dance parties for their friends, starring her collection of vintage records.

The next weekend they were parking it by the barn behind their historic stone house and stringing it with Christmas lights. Soon, it became the perfect guesthouse while renovations were carried out on their home. With Lizzie's artful touches, the Bambi became a 1960s masterpiece and their friends, including many celebrities, were asking if they could "sleep outside in the trailer."

Now, it's the star of their backyard, serving as the perfect dance hall. Lizzie, daughters Mia and Ava, and anyone else who wants to join in, can climb inside, turn on the tunes, and sing and cut up for hours. During summer afternoons with friends, Lizzie puts out what she calls her "craft services"—movie lingo for the people responsible for coffee, beverages, and snacks on the set. On the afternoon of these photos, she served up a *Sopranos* tribute—a scrumptious cake sent from friend James Gandolfini on a vintage plate given to her by her sister, Lorraine Bracco.

Aidan has played opposite the biggest stars in Hollywood—from Meryl Streep to Julia Roberts to Brad Pitt—but the sparkle in his trademark blue eyes isn't from the dazzle of Hollywood, it's from the fabulously fun girls in his life who take him dancing in his own backyard.

The interior of the Bambi was perfectly preserved. Lizzie decorated it with treasures from the 1960s she'd found over the years, including a velvet Elvis and a stamp collection her friend Kathleen gave her, featuring a stamp from every state.

The family loves to spin vinyl on a new "old" record player Lizzie bought at Renovation Hardware. Her favorites include hits of the 1950s and 1960s like "Moon River," "The Lion Sleeps Tonight," "Mack the Knife," and anything by Elvis, Bob Dylan, or The Beatles.

The Quinns' youngest daughter, Mia (above right), loves to play with friends in the Airstream, and is pictured here showcasing her mom's Elvis collection with friend Asia. The girls spent the rest of the afternoon collecting milkweed "snow" to toss in the air at the dance party.

Aloha Hawaii

Owner: Carey Hultgren
Location: Sonora, California
Model: 1973 Ambassador

Carey Hultgren found both her loves at first sight. The silver one she saw sitting on the side of the road at a garage sale with a sign in the back window: "$2,000 OBO." And the handsome one she bumped into in a bookstore while on vacation with her parents.

After spotting the silver one, a 1973 Airstream International Ambassador, she obsessed all night to the handsome one, fiancé Randy Davis, that someone was going to get to the garage sale the following morning before she did. Randy was hesitant as they drove in the pre-dawn hour to be first in line at the garage sale. This Airstream sounded a bit like the one he had lived in for five years as a teenager and he didn't know if he wanted to do it again. But he knew Carey had dreamed of owning one since childhood and two hours later, after making her best offer of $1,200, they were towing it home.

Interior designer Carey Hultgren, pictured here with fiancé Randy Davis, used her Airstream as both an interior design thesis project and as a temporary home. Though currently parked on a country lot on the outskirts of Sonora, California, according to records, the Ambassador has been as far as New Zealand, with second owners, caravanners Hal and Lucy Young.

Upon closer inspection away from the frenetic energy of the garage sale, Carey discovered the interior was in pretty bad shape. The foam cushions, beds, window fittings, and many other items were "disgusting," never having been replaced in the trailer's three-decade history. "She was filthy," Carey reports. "There were cigarette butts behind the sofa and gummy tar everywhere."

Though she only had $1,500 in savings and most of her fellow students did their projects only theoretically, on paper, Carey told her interior design professor that she'd found her thesis project. She was going to design a small space, her "dream trailer." "The best thing about an Airstream," she wrote in her project diary, "is that you can do anything. Go completely insane and it can never be too much. You can experience it all in one deep breath."

Carey had trouble making up her mind on the style. She was obsessed with the 1950s at the time, had always worn vintage dresses, and collected atomic dishware and 1950s patterns, but didn't know

The walls in the lounge and kitchen are painted with stripes of "dill pickle green" and "mayonnaise," and the couch was reupholstered with bold Hawaiian barkcloth.

When she bought it, the exterior was in such good shape, Carey didn't expect the renovation to be a big deal, but after spending an entire year repairing, ripping out, and replacing, Carey became so frustrated she was tempted to hook it to the jeep and tow it back to the site of the garage sale where she bought it.

Inspired by a trip to Hawaii, Carey named her trailer "Maile"—after the tropical leaf used to make leis—and decided she'd remodel the trailer in a Hawaiian theme.

Using $121 worth of barkcloth that she'd bought in Hawaii, Carey did her own reupholstering, even adding whimsy to the toilet seat cover, and picked out complementary retro accessories. Fiancé Randy helped with all the carpentry, covering the walls with grass mats and hanging the bamboo blinds.

if that was right for the Airstream. She kept the faith (thanks to having to report to her professor) during the difficult demolition. It was a birthday trip to Hawaii that gave her the inspiration she was looking for. She decided to take Hawaii back and stuff it into the Airstream. She bought fabric, hula girls, bamboo, and named her Airstream "Maile" (pronounced mai'leh) after the leaf used in leis.

The result was a remodel rather than a restoration. "I made it something completely different because I was obviously craving the tropics in my life." And her 29-footer became a tropical oasis, winning her an "A" in class and fulfilling her childhood dream, as well as starting an addiction. "Maile" now has a sister in the yard...a 1976 Safari...and Carey might need an inspirational trip to Africa.

Leaning Pine

Owner: Gregory Coster
Location: Kingston, New York
Model: Airstream Sovereign

"I never saw an Airstream in England," Clare Helen Kelly explains, "but I did know of a few people who'd just show up at your house and start living there!" It's a crisp fall morning, and she and husband David Barra are sitting in front of a Sovereign that isn't theirs, roasting marshmallows and playing the guitar.

The owner, art dealer Gregory Coster, is away on an art quest to the nether regions of the world, leaving his Airstream at his sprawling haven at one of the most precious times of the year, a time when the leaves create their own priceless work of art, an inimitable calico mural. "The Admiral," as Gregory is known by friends, kindly asked his friends David and Clare to "keep an eye on the place."

Sitting amid the pines on a brisk fall morning roasting marshmallows and playing guitar is about as close to heaven on earth as it gets, according to David Barra and Clare Kelly. The couple, who own their own Airstream, regularly visit the Sovereign at their friend Gregory's lake house in order to keep the silver beauty company while Gregory travels the world on art quests. One of his finds, a sculpted metal flag by artist Bates Wilson, salutes the change of seasons.

"I fell in love with Airstreams the first time I saw them," Clare remembers as she pulls a gooey marshmallow from its stick and offers it to her husband. "And the fact that our friendship with Gregory resulted in getting one of our own is even better." David, a dimensional stone fabricator and architectural woodworker, met Gregory when he was commissioned to do some work on the Admiral's estate, a magical place called Leaning Pine, 90 miles north of New York City on Dewitt Mills Lake. While David was working at the house, he and the Admiral became friends. The Admiral greatly admired David's craft, and David admired the Admiral's eclectic art collection, including his 1976 22-foot Overlander, so a deal was made—the Admiral would get new granite countertops from David and, since he had two Airstreams, David would get his Overlander.

Shortly thereafter, Clare graduated from Smith College, and she and David started building a house. Not just any house—an environmentally friendly, energy-conscious, steel and concrete home with a sod roof. In the early stages of construction they lived in their Airstream, and then they loaned it to a friend and his wife to live in while they built their house, which brings us full circle back to Leaning Pine and the lovely fall morning in the woods, roasting marshmallows, and playing guitar.

An early ad for Airstream promised buyers a "home away from home." Sometimes Airstreams can serve as a home while you're building a home, a home for others while they're building a home, or as a secret getaway when others are away from home…just ask Clare Kelly and David Barra. Airstreams for them are like campfires, marshmallows, and good music—meant for sharing.

All the comforts of home, perhaps even more. The spacious interior, preserved and in good condition, features a large bathroom, adjacent to the bedroom, with separate shower and toilet. The convenient galley kitchen has an extra-large work area, apartment-size Magic Chef stove, and a Royal Dometic refrigerator.

Keeping the original woods and adding plush fabrics and a cozy velvet armchair make this Sovereign the perfect guesthouse getaway for visiting friends, especially with its special sliding door for bedroom privacy. The silver-rimmed windows frame the views of the ducks floating atop Dewitt Mills Lake.

Silver Jewel

Owner: Kristiana Spaulding
Location: Lotus, California
Model: 1967 Airstream
Tradewind

When artist Kristiana Spaulding needs inspiration she heads inside her 1967 Tradewind. The small space, she says, allows for creativity and stimulation unlike other spaces because it is easily transformed with color, shapes, or even a mood. Kristiana first saw an Airstream when she was seven years old during a monthlong cross-country trip with her family from New York to California in a Volkswagen bus. She marveled at the colors it reflected in its silver exterior as it moved down the highway and how she could wave to herself as their VW bus drove alongside.

Years later, after graduating from New York University, Kristiana once again headed cross-country to get her master's degree in sculpture from the Academy of Art College in San Francisco. She worked for room and board in a residence hotel, all the while fantasizing about having her own apartment someday. She began creating the perfect apartment in miniature inside a small vintage suitcase and carrying it back and forth with her to class.

Jewelry designer and fine artist Kristiana Spaulding splits her time between San Francisco and a small town in the foothills of the Sierras. After purchasing the trailer from a cowboy in Idaho, she did a custom renovation on it and now opens it to the public every October during San Francisco Open Studios.

"K's silver trailer interior," redesigned and constructed by Kristiana with furniture constructed by architect Pierre Maury of San Francisco. She's fond of functional art, like the sink countertop covered in postcards she has received from friends all over the world, immortalized as decoupage.

One day, the postman saw her putting her wallet inside the suitcase and caught a peek at the intricately designed room settings neatly tucked inside. "Your little home away from home," he said with a smile as he handed her a stack of mail.

"Exactly!" she remembers thinking. "A home away from home." And that's when her mind landed on an Airstream. Like her suitcase, it was a way to travel accompanied by her sentimental objects and her art. She could just make them portable. She decided that for her master's thesis she'd rent an Airstream so she could present her sculptural work within it. It seemed perfect—a tiny home away from home; it was silver, like much of her work; and it's one of the greatest sculptures of modern times.

She found her trailer on a road trip to Idaho with her boyfriend. It was owned by a woodworking cowboy named Archie who had a horse that thought she was a dog. Archie had lived in the Airstream

while building his just completed house, and he (but not the horse) was ready to let it go. Though she could hardly believe she was doing what she found herself doing, Kristiana wrote him a check and they towed the Airstream back to California.

The transformation of the interior was as exciting for the young artist as any piece she'd created. "I got to take a beautiful form," she says, "and make it more beautiful." The outcome has been a big hit. Besides using the Tradewind as an Open Studio, she's launched a website, a trailer jewelry line, and a collection of housewares. Now that's silver inspiration.

Kristiana was sketching trailers long before she got one of her own. The abstract oval with little tire was an icon promise to herself that she'd one day own one. Her line of jewelry and miniature sculptures touches upon the familiar and the comical, often with inspiration coming from sentimental objects. (Available at www.silvertrailer.com.)

Kristiana's "Room Settings," are narrative living spaces of places she has inhabited throughout her life, and her "Wearable Essentials" are her travel-related jewelry—jewelry that is intended to be worn with self-sufficiency in mind.

Edison

Owner: The Welschmeyers
Location: Niles, California
Model: 1958 Traveler

Within the first hour of owning their silver trailer, architect Paul Welschmeyer and his two sons, Mike and Eric, had stripped it down to the aluminum shell without so much as snapping a "before" picture. They didn't know then that it was a 1958 "Traveler," one of only a hundred trailers made of that style; all they knew was that the interior was rotten and disgusting. "A vicious roadkill would summon a similar emotion," the architect says, "and no one would consider taking a picture of that!"

Traditionalists close your eyes. In his redesign, Paul was more interested in functional systems than creating a nostalgic showplace. His architectural practice was expanding and he needed a job-site design trailer. At the same time, his two boys were becoming teenagers and he and his wife Jana wanted a way for the family to have fun together. The result, after two years of work, is an incredible space that does double duty as a family vacation home and mobile office.

During the renovations, Jana, an interior designer, dubbed the trailer "Edison" and came up with some clever ideas. The family decided that

The Welschmeyers regularly travel with the Marciniks and their 1962 Bambi and the Dows and their 1964 Globetrotter, including a trip to the set of the Tim Burton remake of *Planet of the Apes* (left). On New Year's Eve 2001, the families (each with two children) journeyed to the Mohave Desert, where the systems were put to the test in the freezing cold. The solar electrical system had to work extra hard during the short daylight hours, but they still managed a showing of *2001: A Space Odyssey* projected onto a white sheet laid over the Marciniks' Bambi.

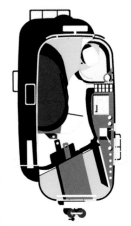

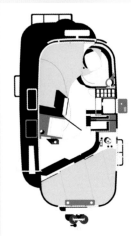

carry-ons must be restricted to one per person, but they also needed a way to store sleeping bags and pillows. Following Paul's "Trailer Tao" principle that everything must have two purposes, Jana designed hollow bolsters, which would store the family's sleeping gear, and also provide all the necessary back support throughout the trailer for the banquettes.

The project has been a huge success, both for the architect and for the family. Paul was awarded the American Institute of Architects' Honor Award for his design (beating out $8 million homes!) and the family has logged 10,000 miles of vacation fun. When not in use as a job-site trailer or vacation home, Edison stays in the backyard like a good dog, awaiting a visit from Paul and Jana anytime they need to escape from a house full of teenage boys.

Architect Paul Welschmeyer says the design was "the hardest and most frightening project" he ever attempted, so he established a "Trailer Tao"—everything must have two or more uses. The banquette, for example, is used as a dining table on vacations and as an office desk on job sites.

Family Fun

Owner: Simon Brown and
Liz Bauwens
Location: East Sussex, England
Model: Flying Cloud II

In the 1960s, during his school days in England, photographer Simon Brown dog-eared the pages of his *National Geographic* magazines, drooling over America's enthusiasm with the space age and the ads for Wally Byam's sleek metallic Airstreams. In the 1990s, as his photography career blossomed, Simon became tech savvy and discovered the Internet. "Since I'm not that mad about porn, I went hunting Airstreams," the photographer laughs. "When I found a 1975 Flying Cloud on the Classic Airstream site, I rang the States to discuss buying it."

The seller happened to be Rockabilly Hall of Famer Matt Lucas, who in the 1960s recorded the hit "I'm Movin' On." For several months Simon chatted with the rocker about Airstreams, music, Elvis (one of the famous musicians for whom Matt had drummed), and then the more practical matter of how to get an Airstream shipped from America to England. For $6,000, Simon bought his dream, and for another $1,500 it became one of the first to be shipped to the UK, where it now sits in a field on the south coast of England.

Simon and his wife, designer Liz Bauwens, outfitted the Airstream for family fun, "sort of Airstream meets *Toy Story*'s Woody," to the delight of their three children, Lois (12), Milo (10), and Finn (7). Finn

As the original fixed table for the dining area was missing, the Browns commissioned a freestanding folding table in a sympathetic style that can be used indoors or out, since they love throwing great raucous outdoor dinner parties for friends. Favorite meals include salmon teriyaki, local organic steak, fresh vegetables, elderflower cordials, ginger beer, and loads of champagne, after which they gather round a fire, singing songs to Simon's guitar and "generally falling over."

The interior design of the Browns' Flying Cloud came from a table lamp featuring children's cowboy cap guns that Simon picked up in a junk store. From there, Liz mixed the nostalgic and the whimsical with some vintage cowboy print cushions from trendy London design shop Cath Kidston. Continuing the Americana theme, the double bed is covered in classic stars and stripes, and the seating area at the door end (which converts to a full bed) was built for the Airstream in the style of an American diner banquette and covered in shiny red leatherette.

Part Two
STYLE STREAMS

"Style is knowing who you are, what you want to say and not giving a damn," said Gore Vidal. Perhaps unlike any other, the self-contained environment of a trailer provides an open canvas to which the artist can apply a diverse palette of textures, patterns, and paints. And whether traditional, contemporary, candy-striped, or polka-dotted, silver trailer owners know their style and express it exactly as they want.

There are so many ways to fulfill the dream you dream inside an Airstream. Traditionalists scour the Internet for original pieces in order to re-create the interior environment exactly as it was, but others hunt for ways to redecorate their homes away from home as completely different worlds unto themselves. They create an altogether new atmosphere that's frisky, fun, and playful.

The best thing about the interior of this space-age wonder is that it's entirely capsulated and versatile, allowing the dreamer to be adventurous and not give a damn. Come be a "trailer tapper," open the door and look inside to see how dreams become silver-styled reality.

RETRO STYLES

This 1936 Clipper, the earliest known to exist, is towed by a 1936 Diamond T "House Car" (complete with bedroom on board). The Diamond T was created by C.A. Tilt for wealthy ranchers in the 1930s, who argued that, "A truck doesn't have to be homely."

What is it about vintage? Why have Airstreams rolled into pop culture in full glory? Perhaps because vintage rekindles nostalgic memories of family trips or youthful experimentations. Or perhaps because silver vintage allows us to salute our quirky, idealistic sides. Or perhaps it's because these *objets d'art* are sturdy, durable survivors, who've waited their return to glory in backyards and junkyards all across America. Waiting to be snapped up and recognized as worthy. Whatever the case, vintage is "in."

The early Airstream sales brochures promised buyers they'd be able to take all the "comforts of home" with them wherever they traveled. Today, eBay proudly boasts item after item of Airstream merch, and entire dealerships have been created to market to the followers. Wally Byam knew his creation would last. He was so confident in his all-metal, all-aluminum construction and all-steel undercarriage that he gave buyers a "Lifetime Guarantee," which reflected his inimitable sense of humor: "Anything that goes wrong that could possibly be our fault will be repaired without charge at the factory for as long as you own your Airstream."

Good to the guarantee, some of the first Airstreams built on a Model A Ford chassis with aircraft aluminum are still on the road. In fact, more than 60 percent of all Airstreams ever built are still streaming down the road. So, if you're looking for a vintage model the good news is that since so many have survived, you probably don't need to take out a mortgage to buy one. But beware, as you'll see on the following pages, some people become so enamored by the mystique of one, they end up with quite a collection....

Granddad

Vince Martinico has been collecting "stuff" since kindergarten—wheat pennies, stamps, firecracker labels, cigar bands, and kites—all because he liked the graphics. By high school he was collecting rock 'n' roll posters, glass doorknobs, and bicycles. As he grew older, his toys got bigger—motorcycles and old panel trucks. But nothing compares to his excitement of being the largest collector of vintage Airstreams in the United States. So big, he's approached Governor Arnold Schwarzenegger about opening a travel trailer museum near Vince's Auburn, California home.

Vince became interested in old travel trailers after seeing an early Bowlus at a car museum. Never one to settle for anything less than the best, Vince acquired what's known as the granddad of all Airstreams, a 1936 Clipper, so named because it is almost a spitting image of the Pan Am Clipper airplane on wheels. Vince's isn't just any 1936 Clipper, it's the earliest one known to exist (#1224), and when he bought it, he discovered through various papers and magazines stored within the revolutionary beauty that it was owned by Wally Byam's neighbors.

Hopefully, they obtained a "good friend discount" because even though the Clipper was introduced during the Great

Named after the TWA Clipper aircraft, the first plane to take people in numbers on a transatlantic flight, the 1936 Clipper is the first Airstream to be mass-produced. This is the interior of the oldest one known to exist, still rust-free thanks to Duraluminum, a lightweight alloy created in 1915 that's as strong as steel but one-third of the weight.

The little boy who started with a childhood collection of wheat pennies is today the largest collector of Airstream trailers in the United States, with at least 50 of the silver retro beauties at any one time all decked out to the last rivet with museum-quality period pieces.

Vince Martinico keeps about 55 trailers housed in old chicken coops the size of football fields, 35 of which are in his permanent collection and 20 or so he keeps on hand to buy and sell. He's collected and sold every variation of Airstream made from 1936 to 1968, and many of the interiors, like his prized Clipper, are restored (or preserved) perfectly. Who would expect anything else from the man who still has his marbles from childhood?

Depression years, it was quite pricey—$1,200—but apparently worth it. The company couldn't build them fast enough to keep up with demand. With its monocoque, all-riveted aluminum body, it was more like the aircraft of the day than any travel trailer.

Wally (perhaps with help from wife Stella) thought of everything. The Clipper has its own water supply, an enclosed galley, and can sleep four, thanks to a steel dinette that can convert to a bed. The Clipper features electric lights throughout and a superior insulation and ventilation system, even offering dry ice "air-conditioning." These "modern" marvels were manufactured until 1938, when structural aluminum was classified as a critical war material, as it was needed to build aircraft for the looming World War II.

Vince's collection started with a 1947 Silver Streak and includes other industry stalwarts, such as Bowlus and Curtiss, but he likes nothing more than his Clippers. The "kindergarten collector" now has three of the rare originals. Besides #1224, he'll proudly tell you he also owns #1228 and #1232 and that Director Tim Burton, another big fan of the Clipper, has one too, "though his is a higher number." According to Vince, he is willing to let go of trailers when he's "upgrading," but #1224 will "always remain a keeper."

Shady Dell

A stone's throw from the Mexican border in mile-high Bisbee, Arizona, sits perhaps the most adorable trailer park in all of America. Founded in 1927 as a spot where weary travelers could park their trailers or pitch their tents en route east or west on Highway 80, the Shady Dell is today a place where visitors flock to spend a night of nostalgia in refurbished and redecorated trailers that look as perfect now as the day they rolled off the assembly line.

There's quite a silver-sided lineup—everything from a 1954 12-foot Crown that was Earl and Marge's beloved vacation home-on-wheels for more than 40 years to the pinnacle of elegance, Airfloat's "Flagship," an enormous gold 1957 model that new park owners, Laura Chumley and Wesley Barchenger, have just painstakingly restored, complete with Elvis movies on a vintage TV set.

A couple of years back, while in Bisbee to check out a local aviation school Wesley wanted to attend, the couple spent a night at Shady

Laura Chumley and Wesley Barchenger bought Shady Dell, a marvelous piece of Americana in Bisbee, Arizona, after a one-night stay. They offer a sleek lineup of vintage aluminum travel trailers for overnight or weekly rental. The collection, all polished down to the rivets, includes a 1949 Airstream, 1950 Spartanette, 1954 Crown, and a 1951 Royal Mansion. Also on site is Dot's Diner, a 1957 Valentine with 10 stools that serves breakfast and lunch five days a week.

Dell and decided to buy the property. Wesley gave up his job as a mortician in Anchorage, Alaska, and the couple and their three kids moved into Shady Dell. "I didn't know anything about restoring old trailers," Wes laughs. "But when you've restored dead people, well…" The couple quickly made eBay their best friend and have done a terrific job of restoring the park's silver luster.

Interiors are rich woods or polished aluminum, and every effort has been made to keep the décor original. Chenille bedspreads, Formica-topped tables, and vintage dishware bring guests back to carefree days of comfort and family fun. At night, you can curl up on an upholstered sofa and listen to vintage records on old phonographs or watch 1950s television favorites on original black-and-white televisions. Outside each trailer is a grassy yard with lounge chairs.

In the morning, after a cup of percolated coffee, visitors can head to Dot's Diner, an authentic 10-stool diner built in 1957 by the Valentine Manufacturing Co. in Wichita, Kansas. Lovingly restored to its Art Deco splendor, the diner serves Shady Dell guests and townsfolk home-cooked breakfast and lunch every Thursday thru Monday.

And the price for this journey back to the good old days is surprisingly retro, just like the trailers. For $40 a night you can snuggle up in the "Homemade"—a comfy little 10-footer built in 1952 from plans out of *Popular Mechanics*. Or if you feel like a king, splurge and spend $85 for the 1951 Royal Mansion, where you can sip martinis sprawled out on a vintage leopard carpet in the living room.

Whatever your tastes—from nostalgic to kitsch—Shady Dell's trailers will transport you there.

Hawaiian Style

This 1947 Flxible Airporter, formerly the bus for the Sacramento Solons baseball team, has been converted into a Polynesian palace. Accommodations include a kitchen, dining "room," small bathroom, and two beds off the middle aisle. Flxible, a company that originally sold a motorcycle with patented "flexible" sidecar, was forced into the bus market when the Ford Motor Company introduced the roadster for less than the cost of a motorcycle.

Aloha! Slip on your hula skirt, a pair of flip-flops, and crank up the Don Ho, Hawaii has pulled into town. One of the most popular trends over the past few years has been to pack the passport into home décor. Capturing the feel of exotic lands allows you to embark on a vacation without ever leaving home. And who doesn't need a vacation, especially in a muumuu (a word that proves as fun to wear as it is to speak and spell!)?

When decorating Hawaiian style, the more colorful the better, as long as it includes coconuts, pineapples, and hula girls (as well as the occasional parrot). And if the color doesn't look quite right, have another mai tai, and it will! The great thing about decorating with Hawaiian flair is the multiple uses of a variety of everyday items. Printed sarongs can double as tablecloths. Palm fronds create atmosphere and can even be woven together to make functional roofs and windbreak walls. Old travel posters from the 1930s and 1940s can add a faraway flavor, and paper parasols on the edge of a drink will put anyone in a tropical mood.

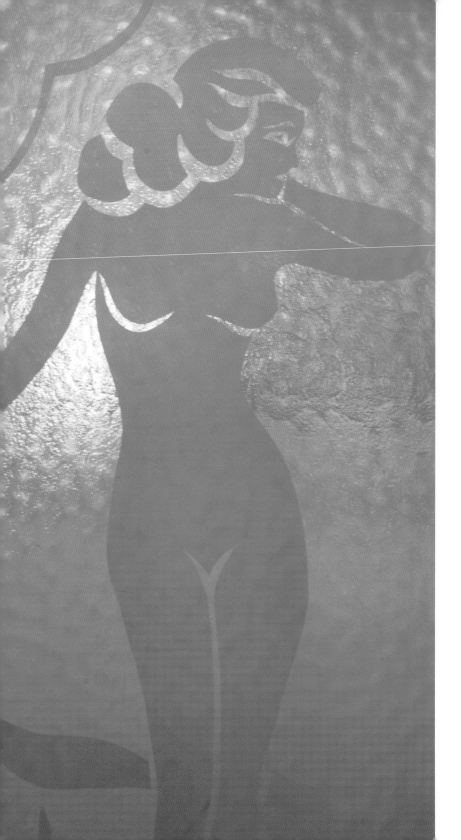

Wonderfully kitschy, retro mod fabrics can brighten any room, especially when adorned with hula girls and ukuleles. Basically, everything will work with Hawaiian-themed décor, as long as it features a palm tree or a Hawaiian hula girl, especially if she wobbles at the waist.

The joy of decorating to a Hawaiian theme is that it makes every day a party, because in Hawaii any excuse for a party is a good reason. Just keep a guitar or ukulele within arm's reach, and an impromptu hula is bound to break out.

Greet your guests at the door with a shell or flower lei and have them leave their shoes at the door! Have a bowl of loose flowers on hand for your guests to tuck behind their ears. If you're "available," put the flower behind your right ear. If you're taken, put it closest to your heart, behind your left ear.

Doris Day Style

With her bright personality and figure to die for, Doris Day set the standard for beauty, class, and sex appeal in the 1950s and 1960s. The wholesome movie star and singer defined a playful, innocent time, in which sex appeal came not from baring all, but by delivering a perky attitude and feminine elegance. Doris Day had the persona that men loved and women respected. If you always wanted to be Doris Day (or marry her), you can live the life you dreamed by dolling up your trailer with some vintage delights.

When searching for a 1950s-girl motif, "Perhaps, perhaps, perhaps," reach for fabrics and memorabilia reminiscent of Day's cheerful style perfection—a time of doing things for your own reasons and not someone else's, of looking for love in all the right places, and, most of all, a time that was spicy enough not to be taken too seriously.

Even a cup of coffee is romantic when made with an Art Deco, United chrome coffee percolator with Bakelite handles; and accents like a vintage chalkware wedding cake topper and rhinestone-

Memorabilia, illuminated by a period sconce, includes the 1949 magazine advertisement, above, proclaiming the beauty and value of the "new" Motorola portables. Motorola, currently a big name in cell phones, offered its "glamorous" AC/DC and battery-operated radios at prices between $19.95 and $49.95 for the "luxury" model.

A 1950s diner table, set with vintage flatware and bubblegum pink Melmac dinnerware made by Arrowhead in Cleveland is ready for a romantic rendezvous. A colored aluminum cup as shiny as the ceiling poses as a neat vase.

encrusted clock are amusing pieces that might get a conversation started. A photo album of vintage wedding pictures and a record player with a large selection of 45s—Elvis, Pat Boone, Vic Damone, and, yes, Doris Day adds to the ambience.

With its curved ceiling at each end, steel cupboards, and wood cabinets, this 21-foot 1949 Airstream was ready to come of age in 1950s fun. Bright and cheery accents create an atmosphere of sensual innocence that might turn a "perhaps, perhaps, perhaps" into a "yes, Yes!, YES!" The inviting chenille-covered bed and the Airstream's polished aluminum ceiling may further inspire getting a little loving started and reflect a time to remember. So, whether it's the charm of your wedding night or the scandal of a ribald affair, it would certainly be fun to set it in Doris Day innocence. And, as they say, if the trailer's rockin', don't come a knockin'!

The sexy, clean lines of this 1949 Airstream ceiling reflect the fun happening below. A vintage chenille bedspread with a pair of peacocks, a bejeweled Phinney-Walker German clock, and a chalkware bride-and-groom cake topper mirror an era of pink purity.

Tex-Mex Style

Think "Tex-Mex," and you usually think tacos, chili, and salsa. "Tex-Mex travel" probably conjures up visions of a wagon pulled by a team of burros, certainly not the interior of a silver travel trailer. As for "Tex-Mex style," you could be forgiven for thinking it an oxymoron!

Those loud colors and primitive objects made in Mexico and the Southwest have long been considered anything but stylish. But suddenly the style is hotter than a tamale, because it's simple, accessible, and colorfully delightful—not to mention extremely affordable. And these days the utilitarian objects and vivid colors are finding their way into contemporary homes and, yes, even travel trailers.

Designers around the world have discovered that Tex-Mex style works perfectly inside entire homes or small spaces because of its vibrancy, its no-frills practicality, and its quality handcrafted workmanship. What exactly is Tex-Mex style? And why can it live side by side with either contemporary pieces or with Americana antiquities?

Tex-Mex design is a celebration of a rugged, romantic beauty and rich history of people working with their hands and the land to create simple and functional elements using organic objects and natural dyes. The hand-carved, brightly painted furniture remains underpriced, considering the quality and ingenuity, and the palette of colors is so visually appealing that even the mundane takes on a newfound excitement.

Most of all, Tex-Mex style has a flavor all of its own. It makes you feel good, like an afternoon siesta. So, grab a margarita and relax in a sense of comfort and local history that have survived the test of time.

This snug little 10-foot travel trailer, built in 1952 from plans featured in *Popular Mechanics*, comes to life with the colors of Mexico and the Southwest. Tex-Mex adds character to any space and creates a happy glow, like a rich Mexican sunset.

These cheerful homemade curtains crowned with carved wooden valances make use of long-neglected Mexican textiles, and the table is set with vintage Colorflyte cups and saucers by Branchell. The cute Mexican figurine and reproduction Crosley radio were found on eBay.

Late Art Deco Style

The interior of this 1951 33-foot Royal Mansion feels stately, with its breakfast booth and living room, complete with vintage phonograph and a selection of Josephine Baker records. The refrigerator is a Frigidaire, made exclusively by General Motors, and the cabinets and cupboards in pale veneered woods and handles with clean lines define the Moderne movement.

Born in the Roaring Twenties, the Art Deco movement grew out of the social and economic depression and all-around graveness of the war years. Art Deco (as it's known today) was a style of optimism and prosperity. People wanted a "modern," functional style and Art Deco was the exuberant reaction, particularly in Paris. During this time, the Charleston and tango became the latest dance crazes, jazz was born, and Greta Garbo and Marlene Dietrich sizzled on the silver screen. And amazingly, to the credit of its indomitable spirit, Art Deco style not only survived the Great Depression, it thrived.

Designers were inspired by ancient Egypt (the Tutankhamun Exhibition was held in Paris in 1922) and also the streamlined designs of ocean liners and industrial machinery. The designs were geometric, clean, and unfussy, and traditional materials were rejected in favor of

more exotic materials like chrome, plastics, ebony, and animal skins. Art Deco furniture was made to the highest and most luxurious standards, using rare woods and veneers.

Inspired by the pyramids, glamorous "stepped-up" buildings appeared as zigzag silhouettes in the skylines around the world, including New York landmarks such as the famed Chrysler Building, Empire State Building, and Radio City Music Hall, and helped skyscrapers reduce their ground area as they grew taller in order to allow sunshine to peek between buildings.

After the Wall Street Crash of 1929, money evaporated and the need for cheaply made merchandise grew. Extravagant decoration gave way to simplicity: designs featuring parallel lines and rounded corners that facilitated machine mass production and cheap prices. Art Deco became the first high fashion adapted for the assembly line and it spread throughout almost every aspect of life, streamlining everything from fashion to automobiles.

Interestingly, Wally Byam's design for his earliest trailers were self-described as "boxy structures," but by the time he introduced the Clipper in 1936 (in the latter days of the Art Deco movement) it was so streamlined it looked like the Pan Am Clipper on wheels. And Wally chose as his first tow vehicle the Chrysler "Airflow," a car that defined the late Art Deco aesthetic.

Today, the machine-age good looks of Art Deco designs are again in hot demand. If imitation is the highest form of flattery, the pioneers of the movement would feel venerated, if not entertained, by all the repros, knockoffs, and imitations.

This "vintage" Art Deco chrome and plastic radio, above left, is actually a Teac reproduction, featuring a CD player and AM/FM radio behind its parallel lines and streamlined looks. The covered fruit bowl, left, is by Lane & Company, Van Nuys, California.

Lighting with a stepped profile is the epitome of the Moderne shape, and features chrome, a brand-new material during the Art Deco period. The leatherwork is by Kelly Humphrey and Brad Overacker at Va Voom! in Bisbee, Arizona.

CONTEMPORARY STYLES

The twenty-first century has brought ultramodern amenities to trailer design. Wally's wife Stella may not have gone camping without a stove, but do any of us believe that today she'd be demanding amenities like hydraulic actuators or lubricant dispensers?

Wally Byam cooked up the first space-age, aerodynamic Airstream as "little more than a bed you could crawl into, a shelf to hold a water bottle, a flashlight, and some camping equipment..." And from then until recently the gleaming exterior remained, but the interior design went from "modern" to "has been," tending toward boring beige and bland cream-colored carpeting. The space-age look aged along with the buying demographic.

But all that has changed. The World War II generation, who have for so long dictated the size and styling of many motor homes, is taking a backseat to an eager, design-conscious, adventurous set who are bending ears and changing the paradigm. Today, Airstream design has headed back to the future. The new team at Thor Industries, the maker of Airstream, is hip, cutting-edge, and listening to their fan base. And chic architects and designers from around the world, like San Francisco's Christopher Deam and Dutch-based Atelier Van Lieshout, are catching on that the Airstream interior is a blank silver canvas and there is a younger generation that wants vintage space-age cool for new adventures from mountain biking, surfing, and snowboarding to impressing the design-conscious client. Airstream is not just for your grandpa anymore.

Okay, enough already. Imagine yourself in whichever contemporary, cutting-edge design feels right for you and your adventures. Whether it's the innocent, beach-going fun of a "Quiksilver" Bambi or the raw functionality of Bais-o-drome, rest assured contemporary designers are thinking lifestyle for the twenty-first-century space age. Oh, would Wally flip his beret.

Retro Modern Living

When the designers at Powell & Bonnell Design in Toronto wanted to showcase their talents and problem-solving expertise at the Toronto Interior Design Show, they took a vintage Airstream and created within it a modern oasis of calm and luxury.

At the fore, they designed a dining/work area with a cocktail bar that seats six comfortably, leading to a spatially compact kitchen, featuring mahogany, steel, and granite. Beyond the kitchen, separated by a privacy curtain, is a sleeping/study space designed for day and nighttime use, containing two mohair-upholstered beds, with 6-inch flat-screen televisions and adjustable writing tablets and reading lamps.

Even though it was housed inside a garage during the renovation, the designers used to sit for hours inside their creation and enjoy the view. The retro modern beauty is now owned by a wealthy Texas land developer who loves it so much he keeps it in a climate-controlled storage facility in a state of suspended animation.

From the aircraft-inspired storage bulkhead in the kitchen to the luxurious curved banquette, which has the feel of a vintage Thunderbird, the interior aesthetic of this 1972 Land Yacht evokes the Airstream's curvaceous shell. Rich materials such as shimmering glass tiles, dark-stained mahogany, and stainless steel give a modern slant to the Airstream's essentially nostalgic character.

Love Shack

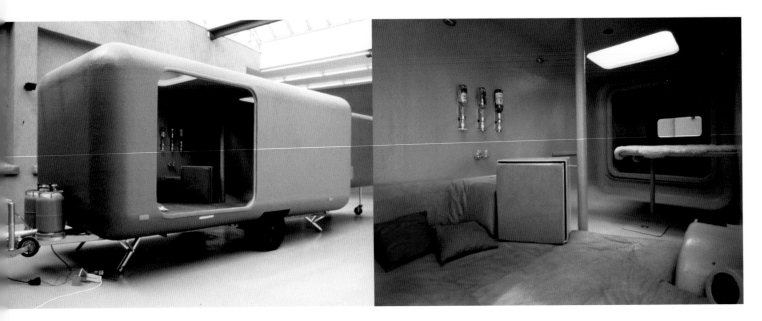

Other Airstream-inspired trailers have entered the design arena with special purposes all their own. (Read no further if your idea of "contemporary style" doesn't include s-e-x.) Dutch Company Atelier Van Lieshout's works, from sculpture to complete architectural refurbishments, are produced by a creative team and intended to suit an "independent lifestyle." The team has built on the success of their 1998 "Commune Bed"—a bed large enough to accommodate a full-blown orgy—by rolling into the twenty-first century with the "Bais-o-drome," a funky mobile home dedicated to "loving."

Bais-o-drome is French high-school slang for an especially orgiastic make-out party, and, quite frankly, it's no accident that this bedroom on wheels shares that name. The Bais-o-drome was built to accommodate cavorting. In fact, Austin Powers might call it the "Shagmobile," since each and every feature within this bedroom on wheels is meant to facilitate a good roll in the...trailer.

Dutch Company Atelier Van Lieshout has created a polyester trailer that might send the faint of heart reeling. The Bais-o-drome's central feature is a voluptuous bed draped in furry blankets and littered with sensually fluffy pillows. Lining the sides are holsters carrying an array of pornographic magazines and a medley of sex toys. An assortment of drink and drugs to move the fun along can be found in the minibar, a treasure trove of mood-altering concoctions, which is always within arm's (or flailing leg's) length.

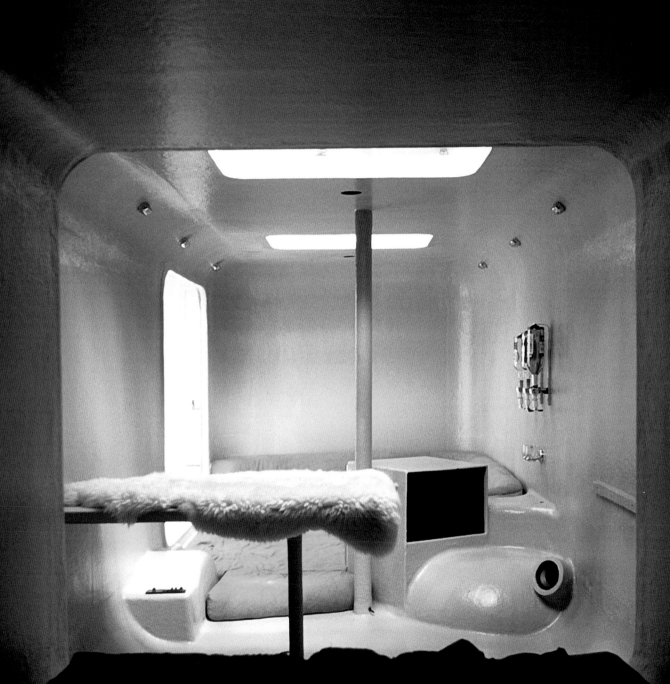

Bachelor Pad

When a wealthy New York bachelor decided to personalize his brand-new Airstream, he hired award-winning designer Alexia Kondylis to give the 30-foot trailer a modern polish. He knew she was accustomed to high-end New York homes. Alexia's dad is celebrated New York architect, Costas Kondylis, and she was fresh from creating the model residence for the Grand Beekman, the first new condominium in the Beekman Place area of the city in more than 25 years. He also knew that in 1999 Alexia was named the Best Young Designer by the Council of Fashion Designers in America and that her work spanned from the classically traditional to the cutting-edge contemporary. But what could she do for his Airstream?

Alexia decided to keep the layout, but immediately scrapped all the factory-installed fabrics and finishes. She then grabbed some of the contractors already working on the bachelor's posh Southampton, New York, farmhouse and set them to work inside the Airstream.

This Airstream serves as a well-appointed guesthouse and, at times, as a hospitality suite at the owner's polo field in Southampton, New York. Each decision in the redesign of the interior was based on personalization. For example, the beadboard in the kitchen was chosen to match the cabinetry in the owner's farmhouse.

Designer Alexia Kondylis customized a brand-new $60,000 Airstream for a New York bachelor. In the living area, she reupholstered the standard-issue sleeper sofa in cotton twill and paired it with a walnut-and-leather safari chair. She chose 2½-inch oak boards to replace the original gray nylon carpet.

Alexia swapped the two twin beds that came factory-installed in the Airstream with a full bed, and created more of a real bedroom feel with sophisticated sconces, rich fabrics, and framed family photos. In the bathroom, she gave the space a clean, masculine touch by attaching strips of teak to the original white acrylic shower wall and upgrading the fixtures.

The electrical, plumbing, and septic systems were new, so Alexia was able to go straight to the good stuff—floors, walls, furnishings, and fixtures. She switched the gray nylon commercial-grade carpet for oak plank flooring and added wainscoting to the cabinetry, which matched the cupboards from the farmhouse. She gave the cabinets an elegant, modern feel with pulls and hardware from Urban Archaeology.

In the living area, she gave the standard-issue sleep sofa a makeover, exchanging the beige chenille with a camel-colored cotton twill and squaring off the overstuffed cushions. In the bedroom, at the other end of the trailer, she replaced the two twin beds with a more guesthouse/bachelor-pad-appropriate full bed, which she covered in masculine linens. To complement the other woods she was adding in the trailer, she added a wooden headboard, which wraps around the top of the bed as a shelf for books, photos, and late-night snacks. And in the bathroom, she covered the prefab white acrylic shower with strips of water-durable teak.

Knowing that all that wood would double the weight of the Airstream, Alexia made the owner promise it was going to remain on his property, so she was shocked to get a call from him shortly after the project was completed saying the trailer worked great on the beach. But your property isn't on the beach, Alexia told him… Oh, he wasn't at his house, he'd towed the trailer 20 miles from his house to a Montauk motel and was thrilled to report that everything was still intact and that people loved it.

And how did Alexia like working on an Airstream? The designer famous for residential buildings, hotels, health clubs, and luxurious homes caught the silver bug. She's just finished restoring the interior of what she calls the "Elvis Presley of trailers," her own 1971 Silver Streak, as a studio in the garden of her barn.

Green Room

There's still much debate in the theatrical world about how the backstage area where performers await their cues became known as the "green room." Was it because the walls were painted green to soothe Shakespearean actors' eyes before the limelight? Or was it because shrubbery was stored there, making the room cool and comfortable? One thing is for certain—the room many celebrities now ask for is silver—Airstream silver.

This Airstream 290, designed by Russel and Marcella Porcas, has appeared in numerous television shows, from *Life and Times of Peter Sellers* to *Too Posh to Wash* with Kim and Aggie, but its main role is as a luxury suite for celebrities, while they're waiting to shoot commercials, music videos, or perform live. Recently, it's even provided a rest area for David Beckham, Michael Owen, and other members of the England soccer team.

Who cares how it became "green?" It now comes in silver!

At Glastonbury Music Festival, the BBC uses an Airstream 290 as a "green room" for all the musicians to do interviews in before going on the main stage. Kylie Minogue favors its comfort and functionality when she's on location because she can warm up, rest, have meetings, and get her hair done without ever leaving the capsule.

As a green room on wheels, this Airstream offers an amazing amount of interior space. It includes a roomy seating area, a makeup chair, modern conveniences like television and coffeemaker, as well as sound equipment and its own generator.

Ralph Lauren

After his friend Nina Hyde, the former fashion editor of the Washington Post, succumbed to breast cancer, designer Ralph Lauren began a foundation to benefit medically underserved persons suffering from cancer. And when he wanted something special, something uniquely American, to design and sell to benefit the foundation, he chose another American legend, Airstream.

He and his creative team recently took four vintage Airstreams to Ralph's Colorado ranch and meticulously decorated them, each in a distinctive theme celebrating American heritage: Adirondack Caravel, Western Bambi, Nautical Bambi, and the Utility/Surplus Airstream.

The Adirondack is ready for a weekend jaunt to the mountains or lakeside with the right balance of country living and refinement, from a buttery leather sofa to a hickory armchair. The Western has a honey-colored knotty pine interior trimmed with barn wood and includes a leather-cushioned bullhorn armchair and whipstitched leather bed.

The man who redefined American style (starting with his signature neckties four decades ago) has done it again. These four Airstreams sold for $150,000 each, proving that the name Ralph Lauren, like the name Airstream, is a legend.

Inspired by a luxury yacht, the Nautical is lined with gorgeous mahogany and comes with teak ocean liner deckchairs and a navy-and-white striped awning. And in the Utility/Surplus, Ralph shows his appreciation for the multipurpose functionality of military gear with stainless-steel floor and walls and olive-painted metal drawer faces.

"Back when all this started, I felt sure that there were no boundaries for Polo," designer Ralph Lauren says of his Airstream adventure. "I'm even more sure of that today."

Ralph Lauren and his creative team meticulously designed vintage Airstreams around four unique themes: Western, Nautical, Adirondack, and Utility/Surplus. Each possesses its own personality and unique style, from cowboy to sailor to sergeant to trailsman.

Part Three

AIRSTREAM PLUS

Moonlighting. Many Airstreams are finding second jobs. They're forgoing careers as destination-bound travel trailers and reinventing themselves as destinations unto themselves. Since the 1960s, when Airstreams were used as mobile quarantine facilities for NASA's Apollo space program, Airstreamers have found unique and creative commercial uses for the sleek recreational vehicles.They've been converted into diners, bars, real estate offices, hair and makeup salons, and even mobile television studios.

And the idea is contagious. Donald Trump's popular reality show *The Apprentice* recently challenged contestants to create a mobile business venture using an Airstream. The results: a sidewalk spa, and an audition booth where aspiring actors can meet casting directors. Airstreams are an instant conversation piece, and no matter what the product, the silver trailer takes the business to a new level of cool. They're flashy, interesting, and pull people to them like a billboard with wheels. Just look inside....

Restaurants and Bars

Silver Streak Bar

This is how my personal silver trailer dream goes....

It didn't cross my mind when we announced we were opening a restaurant with the "World's Only Airstream Bar" that we didn't yet own an Airstream, I just loved the idea of it. But as the calendar ticked toward our grand opening, I realized Airstreams were no longer waiting to be discovered in every open field. I frantically checked eBay, placed "Airstream Wanted" ads, and made calls all over the country, only to find every one of my efforts met with disappointment: "Too far." "Too big." "Ten thousand too much!"

Harry, the soft-spoken contractor who was painting my kitchen at the time, overheard one of my desperate calls. "I've got one," he said. "It's at Sis's house." My head spun around faster than a rotary polisher. That night, after his sister agreed to let go of her "piece of nostalgia," Harry called to say it was mine for the only-in-the-country price of $400. The next week, we snuck the nonroadworthy giant behind his pickup into its place in the garden behind our building, and began

The original Rosendale Cement Company supplied the cement that is the foundation of some of America's most lasting landmarks, including the Brooklyn Bridge and the Statue of Liberty. The Rosendale Cement Company restaurant has become famous for its award-winning food and festive outdoor Silver Streak Bar, overlooking the banks of the Rondout Creek in New York's Catskill region. There, it's always a party.

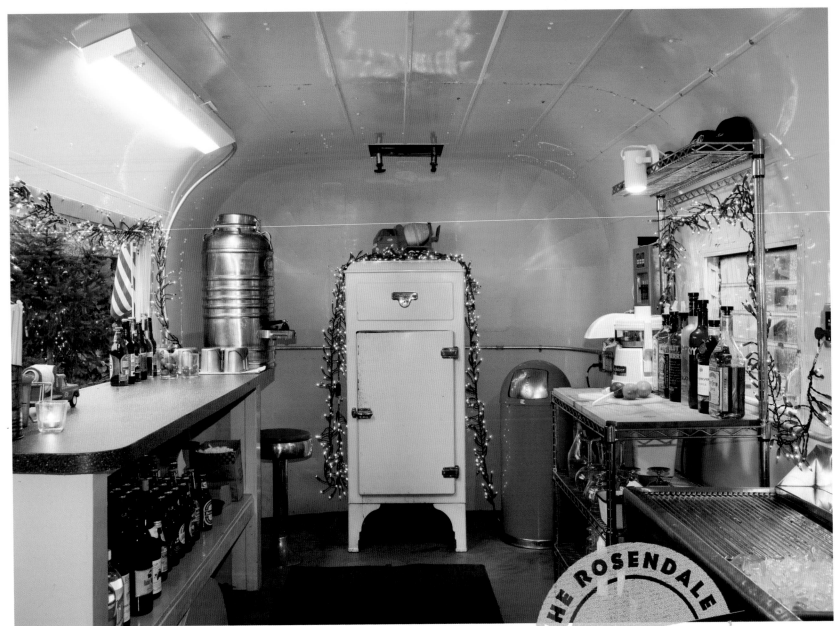

Painted with a bright interior and strung with festive lights, the 1963 Silver Streak makes the perfect outdoor bar, but during the non-summer months it has other roles in the busy restaurant. In October, it's a séance and tarot card room for Psychic Anita, and in December, it's a silver sleigh for Santa and all his packages.

stripping, retrofitting, buffing, polishing, and then came…the building inspector! "GET THAT TRAILER OFF THIS PROPERTY!" he barked at me. I was offended—not only was it insulting how he implied "low rent" in the way he said "trailer," but I had worked hard to find the "World's Only Airstream Bar."

After much town politicking (and begging), the powers that be ruled that we could keep our Airstream. And so—amidst the award-winning gardens of The Rosendale Cement Company Restaurant—sat "The World's Only Airstream Bar" until I started researching this book and found out everything you could possibly know about Airstreams, including the fact that what sat at our restaurant wasn't an Airstream at all but an Airstream look-alike rival! So…

Come visit us at The Rosendale Cement Company in Rosendale, New York—home to the "World's Only Silver Streak Bar." Okay, so it wasn't made by Wally, but boy do we serve a great drink! (You might even toast Harry—he's Rosendale's new building inspector.)

Top Dog

In 1936, Oscar Mayer had a brilliant idea. He created a giant hot-dog-shaped vehicle, the Wienermobile, in order to advertise his "hot dogs." Soon after, his dogs were famous and everyone wanted to "be an Oscar Mayer Wiener." It was truly clever marketing. Almost 50 years later, Andrea Spaulding told her husband Alan that she wanted to open a restaurant, and while on a vacation drive from Tijuana, Mexico, to Las Vegas, he spotted an Airstream and had a wiener of an idea. It didn't take art school training for Alan to see that the silver Twinkie had the shape of a perfect roll. What did Andrea think about turning an Airstream into a giant mobile hot dog stand? Well, she relished the idea, so Alan quickly sketched out his vision on a piece of scrap paper.

When they returned to their Connecticut home, Alan set about with dogged determination to put his plan in action. After a little scouting, he bought a perfectly sized, but dented, 1963 Bambi for $1,500 from a man in Farmington, Connecticut, and began what sounds like taxidermy—an extensive gutting of the Bambi's interior and a complete repair of its aluminum skin.

With his scrap paper sketch tacked to the wall in his basement, Alan became a mad scientist, cutting and riveting sheet metal to create his frankfurter. Neighbors who visited him quickly dubbed him "the man on a mission" and left him to it, but as the ark took shape, their perspective began to change. They noticed that their affable "crazy" neighbor was having fun like a kid in a toy store, and, like the kids did on my street when my tree house began to take shape, one by one they began to offer their assistance and expertise to help Alan Spaulding fulfill his dream.

After retrofitting the interior of the Bambi as one big kitchen and painting the outside red, Alan towed his "Top Dog" stand to a roadside spot near their house in order to see if the crowds liked

Located on Route 66 in Portland, Connecticut, Top Dog is a 1963 Airstream Bambi. It was customized by Alan Spaulding after his wife Andrea fantasized about opening their own restaurant.

their product and to make back some of his expenses. But the traffic proved too infrequent, and he and Andrea decided not to waste any time. Top Dog needed to move to a better-traveled location. They picked a spot beneath the historic metal-trussed Arrigoni Bridge in Portland, Connecticut, and began to sell lunch to local shoppers and the people running businesses beneath the bridge. It was 1979.

Andrea was determined to make the Top Dog work, even when the other businesses beneath the bridge began to fold. As each business left, so did a few of their lunch customers. "If we'd had a storefront restaurant we couldn't just up and move it," she pointed out. "We'd have been stuck. But with the Airstream, we could just tow it to a new location." So, she went site shopping, looking out for well-traveled, easily accessible locations. And what she found was a site by an old railroad depot in Portland on Route 66.

"I sat on the roadside and counted how many cars went by at midday," Andrea explained. That night at dinner, she reported to Alan how many cars passed per half hour on Route 66, and the next day Alan asked the railroad if they could park Top Dog in their unused parking lot. They've been there selling hot dogs every day since. They haven't missed a single day, even when Alan was enhancing the design to make it look more like his original sketch, and even when a new zoning official tried to shut them down.

For the first three or four years, business was good, but when Alan added the "fixings," things took off. He had long wanted to finish the design according to his original sketch, making the Airstream itself a bun and having a wiener poke out each end, but the busy schedule of running the stand had gotten in the way. In the end, he decided he would have to work around the Tuesday through Saturday, 10 a.m. to 3 p.m. schedule. Each night and on Sundays and Mondays, he worked on the enhancements, and, of course, depended on the kindness of neighbors.

At one point 10 neighbors (almost every man in the neighborhood) were on hand to help lift and bolt in place the bulky 150-pound ends, which Alan had spent many nights in his basement handcrafting out of sheet metal and fiberglass. Even though he had never worked with sheet metal before, he became quite a good "tin knocker" just by trial and error. He bought a hand rivet-gun and riveted the ends together, and his friend who owns an auto parts store gave him technical advice on what kind of fiberglass to use. Local artist Robert Ives helped with the original sign and Jimmy Moore, who owns a local auto body shop and is known as a wizard when it comes to custom detailing on motorcycles, did all the airbrushing.

As the conversion progressed, Alan often had to take the trailer to its spot on Route 66 in a less than desirable form. "One day we went down with only one end," he laughed. "And on another day the ends were just primed. Sometimes it really didn't look very good, but people understood as long as their hot dog was delicious." (They got the wieners from a secret supplier in Maine and created their own special toppings by experimenting until they got something they loved.)

Like any good hot dog, the Top Dog stand wasn't complete without the fixings. To top it off, Alan fashioned the mustard out of construction Styrofoam, and the relish was made of pieces of painted wood screwed to a mesh wire. Once the Top Dog was finished, Alan treated the "hot dog helpers" (the neighborhood gang) to a "Golf Open"—a day of golf and a party at the house, complete with…you guessed it…hot dogs! And over the years thousands of people have flocked to the Top Dog seeking out the perfect wiener served out of the perfect stand, including one new zoning official who tried to shut them down.

Twelve years into their successful business and others wanted to follow suit, but the town had ordinances against drive-in restaurants and roadside stands. When other applications were denied, a new

Each end of the giant frankfurter weighs 150 pounds and was handcrafted from sheet metal and fiberglass. The mustard is made from construction Styrofoam, and the relish from pieces of wood that have been screwed to mesh wire. Customers pay $1.75 for a basic hot dog and can choose from a range of specialty toppings, including the couple's famous "fire chili," at a cost of 15 cents per item.

zoning officer decided Top Dog was against local law and decided to shut them down. Fans of the stand rallied with a petition, and the press stood behind them with articles such as "Mustard's Last Stand!" appearing in seven newspapers and *Woman's World* magazine. The town zoning officer backed down (with ketchup on his face) and encouraged the town's planning authority to write in a grandfather clause so that the Top Dog could continue business as usual.

Never ones to not add a little spice, Alan and Andrea have made a few changes over the years, including the addition of a 1972 Checker Cab (complete with dolled-up mannequin passenger.) And, when they noticed a trend toward spicier foods, they added a "fire chili" to their menu board in addition to the popular mild. And it turned out to be a pretty big hit. In addition to the two types of chili, there are the usual condiment duo (mustard and ketchup), as well as hot relish, fried peppers and onions, sauerkraut, and melted American cheese. The basic hot dog is $1.75, with specialty toppings priced at 15 cents per item. "Though the chili cheese dog is our most popular," Alan says, "the sauerkraut runs a close second."

And just how much have the Spauldings spent on this enterprise? About $10,000 on renovations to the Airstream ("excluding my time," Alan is quick to point out), and about $25,000 on the Checker Cab. And they've had a line for almost 25 years. You do the math. Not a bad investment for a brainstorm written on a piece of scrap paper.

Rock 'n' ROLL

Wally Byam once bragged that with a smile and his Airstream he could get access to the world's most exclusive places—from a parking space in Central Park to a police escort beneath the Arc de Triomphe. Times have changed, and it takes a little more than a smile. But with the right retrofitting, doors do open.

The "Radio Lounge" is a custom-built 31-foot Airstream that's been fitted out as a broadcast studio and hospitality suite, and has been parked at major events around the globe. When the techies at Wired for Sound wanted a unique yet efficient antidote to the typically humdrum remote audio booth, they turned to the retro but modern, unusual but familiar appeal of the Airstream. Shiny, exciting, and sexy, it is raising the profile for broadcasters and their sponsors during remote broadcasts at exciting events.

The Radio Lounge's air-conditioned studio provides plenty of space for all the technical bits a sound engineer could dream of, as well as a living area complete with sofa, desk, and a Poggenpohl kitchen with refrigerator and sink to keep even the most persnickety talent happy. Outside the trailer, a programmable LED sign gives great branding space, and specially designed awnings create a covered patio space for outdoor entertaining.

When you're "ON AIR"-STREAM, you can really rock and ROLL.

Clients as diverse as Pepsi and the BBC have found that a 31-foot silver studio complete with LED billboard tends to get you noticed at any event, but when you also have 360-degree views of the excitement around you as well as a sofa and a refrigerator full of Pimm's, you are probably on your way to a lot of fun.

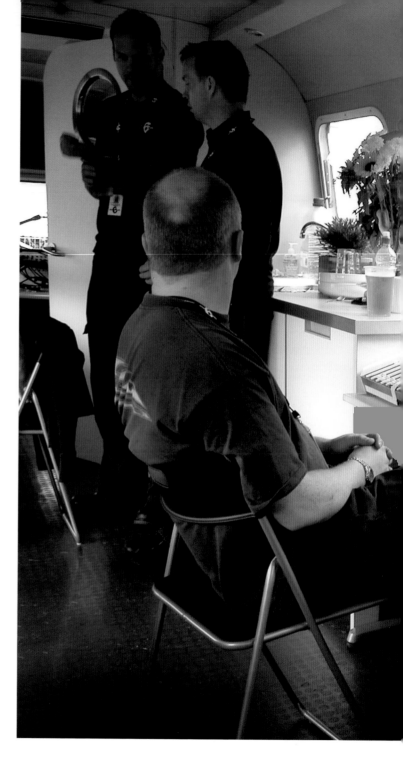

Silver Screen Star

Some have said do what you love and you willl find the road to success. Jason Reed found what he loved to do and that led him to success. But it also led him to love.

In 1994, Jason, then 25 years old, recognized a need within the film industry for location trailers and started his own company, the eponymously named "Jason Trailers, LTD." He realized that for a trailer to be functional for film crews, the interiors needed much more space, and decided the Airstream trailer with its spacious interior and streamlined exterior would be perfect. He found out about two 31-foot Airstreams that were for sale in Melbourne, Florida, and while stateside, he met a "cute girl" named Dana who helped him figure out how to get the silver beasts on a boat and back to Southampton, England.

Jason found his Airstreams unique and filled with character, but discovered that, in his opinion, there was a tragic flaw. The aesthetics of the exteriors of the trailers were sleek and wonderful, but the interiors were dated and in much need of attention. "My goal," he says, "was to bring the feeling of the clean, sleek exterior into the interior of the trailers. I realized they were bland on the inside and that didn't marry with the outside." To complement the modern

Jason Reed brought his shiny-inside-and-out philosophy to his renovation of this Airstream into a five-position makeup trailer. Featured are backlit mirrors, lots of wardrobe space, and leather Wellinda hairstyling chairs that rotate 360 degrees. The countertops are fixed and steel tubular-framed storage shelving was added. Hardwood laminate flooring was installed to cope with the higher traffic demands.

sleekness of the Airstream's exterior, he chose to reline the interior with pre-painted aluminum sheets, and install baseboard trim using hardwearing aluminum diamond plate.

The first trailer was converted into a production/green room and was instantly in demand to be used on several productions. The second Airstream was converted into a five-chair makeup trailer, which could hold up to ten people at a time on location shoots. Details like fixed countertops, tubular-framed storage shelving, hardwood laminate flooring, made the Airstreams functional, and top-of-the-line TVs, stereo systems, and a cappuccino machine made them comfortable.

With the help of Dana, who scoured the trailer parks in Florida, Jason was able to get a steady supply of Airstreams into England, and says that when he called in a silver order, Dana could find a trailer in 24 hours. She helped him find two identical trailers for onscreen roles in Angelina Jolie's film *Lara Croft: Tomb Raider*. Jason's trailers were also used for other productions such as *Evita*, *As Time Goes By*, and *Absolutely Fabulous*. Over the years, the pair shipped more than 20 vintage trailers to England, and they fell in love. Loved lured him to move to the states in 2002, and now, in addition to a marriage and two kids, Jason can be found at the "Trailer Company, Inc." with several trailers in various stages of renovation for rental purposes.

And, yes, like his passion for Airstream trailers, his wedding band is shiny and silver.

The production/green room trailer needed workspace for six people for production. It also needed to have the ability to serve as a lounge area for actors. Both needs were accomplished by designing the desktops to fold down. This allowed extra room for plush furniture to be brought in for resting and lounging. Over the years, his Airstreams were not just behind the scenes. Jason's trailers were seen in several music videos and he provided two identical 31-foot 1970s vintage Airstreams for the action movie *Lara Croft: Tomb Raider* with Angelina Jolie.

Silver Office

When designer Nina Marinkovich and builder Ken Kirsch launched MAK Design & Build, they bought a 22-foot Safari for $7,500 off eBay and created an office that they could take around with them. What they did was instantly establish an identity for the newborn firm.

They chose Airstream because of its look and mobility, but also because it embodies a hip sense of culture and invention. Both Nina and Ken wanted their space to be comfortable, stylish, and functional, and to test and demonstrate green materials in the design (such as bamboo tabletops). "We didn't want to approach the renovations as purists—sorry, Wally!" Nina says. "We were more interested in bridging the old ways of thinking and design principles with new elements and uses for the space."

For that reason, they took out one of the couch/beds and installed the dinette as a place to work and have client meetings. They also incorporated file cabinets into the cabinetry in order to have access to work-related files and display information about the firm for people to see when they walk in.

The Airstream serves as a huge attention-getter when it's parked in its usual location in Ken's driveway, and they've discovered that clients love meeting inside. No, it's not formal, but it sure sets a fun tone.

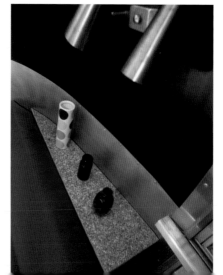

Using eco-friendly building materials like bamboo and Dakota Burl, a composite board made from sunflower seed husks, MAK is able to demonstrate how faster-growing and recycled materials can provide wonderful texture and color, as well as give clients a hands-on demonstration of "green" in action. The interior design echoes the shape and style of the original cabinetry while bringing in a contemporary feel that expresses a more modern aesthetic.

Rolling Art Studio

In search of interesting spaces, both physical and psychological, conceptual land artist Anne-Katrin Spiess has rolled her Airstream into the distant prairies of Nebraska, into the heat and silence of Death Valley, and even to a deserted island in Maine. Often her art exists for only a few hours or days at a time, but before it is disassembled and the landscape is returned to its original condition, she documents it through large-scale photography, video, and text. Besides using her Airstream as an artistic retreat, it's also practical. Inside there's a darkroom and enough supplies for anything her mind can create.

Anne-Katrin sees her Airstream as a "magic little thing" and believes that "optimistic people" own them. As proof, she gives her recent experience of a police escort to a repair shop, offered because she was about to lose a wheel. That's magic that only an artist or an Airstreamer can appreciate.

By creating an art studio inside her 27-foot Airstream, Anne-Katrin Spiess is able to travel with her equipment, books, and art supplies. Within its silver walls, there's a vast amount of storage space, a darkroom, and a living area that is light, encouraging, and versatile. When she's on the road, Anne-Katrin packs enough food, water, and art supplies so that she can go for days without coming into contact with civilization.

What could be more perfect accommodation for a retro-inspired, hip fashion designer and her sculptor husband than a 1946 surf shack and a 1969 Airstream guesthouse? Nothing, so that's why Cynthia Rowley and Bill Keenan sold their million-dollar manse in the Hampton's and moved out to Montauk on the very tip of Long Island to a house 200 yards from the beach. The house was designed as a getaway by Donald Deskey, pioneer of prefabricated housing and iconic packaging for Tide and Crest, and it's so small that Cynthia says she can clean it with a broom in five minutes.

Though the house is aesthetically pleasing to their midcentury modern tastes, they realized they needed a bit more room for weekending guests. So Cynthia rolled into the backyard what she calls "the perfect self-contained environment," a gleaming Airstream Land Yacht. The whole interior design concept is built around letting go of work, and it has everything inside to let guests do just that—from a waxed surfboard to the makings of the perfect cocktail.

If you're lucky enough to get invited for the weekend, ask Cynthia to make you one of her famous "Wet Suits"…a fashionably tasty concoction when you really need to chill. (3 shots light rum, 2 shots Cointreau, 1½ shots fresh lime juice, and slice of orange into a shaker with ice. Shake, and then strain into a sugar-rimmed glass. Sip with style.)

Surf's Up for Cynthia Rowley's Airstream

Designer Cynthia Rowley, known for her cleverly fun fashions, left the headaches of a big house for a tiny surfer's shack on the beach, and she rolled in a vintage Airstream for guests. She used garage sale finds to splash it in a 1960s surfer style that evokes playfulness rather than fanciness.

an endless summer   *montauk pt. long island* 9/26/02

Part Four
FABRICS AND FINISHES

Stripes, solids, plaids, prints. Plastic, wood, vinyl, veneer. Shades, curtains, blinds, drapes. Twin, full, futon, floor. Choices, choices. Each Airstream owner is bombarded with options, starting with the most difficult: "to gut or not to gut" and ending with the most fun: "where shall we go?" It's the gray area betwixt the two that is at times bewitching, at times enjoyable, at times frustrating, but always necessary in order to make it your own.

The great thing is that the Airstream and its interior is entirely versatile—willing to accommodate the boldest of stripes, the splashiest of prints, and small enough that if you don't like it the first time, you can try again. But to save time and money, know what you want before you touch a single rivet. Ask yourself: Who will be doing the work? What will it be used for? When do I need it? Where will it go? Knowing the answers to those questions will help you make the best of your home away from home.

Alternatively, of course, you can dive in like a kid in a sandbox. Dig around for awhile; you're sure to find something you like…

Surfaces

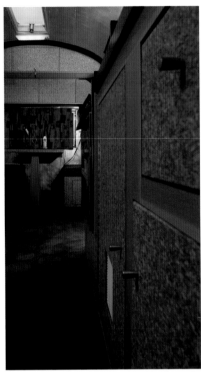

The aluminum and veneer wood surfaces that tend to be factory standard for trailers are chosen for several reasons: they're lightweight, easily cleanable, relatively inexpensive, and vanilla enough that most people don't find them offensive. But when you're making an Airstream your own, you have more options than there are spaces that need surfacing—everything from vinyl to leather, Corian to wood, painted to stripped down to its naked, shiny skin.

Just keep in mind some advice from designers as you consider your options. Your surfaces should be lightweight, if you're traveling; cleanable, if you expect to use it as more than a museum piece; inexpensive, if you're on a budget; and, well, forget vanilla, it's your home on wheels and you can pick chartreuse if that makes you happy.

The surfaces of silver trailers can be adapted to suit a wide spectrum of tastes, which is good news for owners who want an interior with "wow" appeal. The walls can be painted any color you like, or covered in any material—or a variety of materials—including laminates that simulate wood or stone, or even create a postmodern space odyssey. Practical, usable surfaces can be created with vinyl, steel, aluminum, wood, and a myriad of other options.

There are two paths to take within each Airstream—restoration or revamp—and surfaces play a huge role. Traditionalists who "wouldn't change a thing" bring back the factory charm with a combination of original materials and very convincing reproductions. For the rest who aren't committed to restoration, the imagination is the limit and everything from bamboo to Astroturf is within.

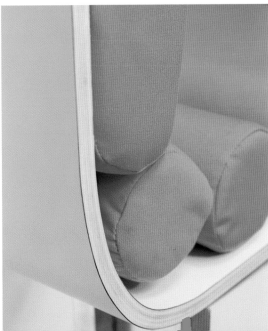

Fabrics

Today there is such a wide array of fabrics to select from, incorporating a host of different fibers, colors, designs, and textures, that the task of picking just the right ones for your Airstream can feel overwhelming. Before you make the first cut, plan ahead. There are a few things you can think through in order to be sure that you'll be stitching pretty.

Inspiration can come from decorating magazines, favorite colors, a memorable vacation, or even a bygone era. Pick based on your personality or theme (and your finances!), but keep in mind that in high-trafficked, high-sun areas, durability should be a key factor in selecting fabrics. In this case practicality wins.

Learn about fabrics. Cotton is extremely strong, is easy care and comes in a vast range of patterns, weights, and weaves. Just note that it wrinkles easily and can shrink, so if you're doing it yourself make sure you prewash. Polyester blends are affordable, wrinkle-resistant, and easy to clean, but don't feel quite as good to the touch as natural fabrics. Wool is resilient, water repellent, and flame resistant, but is susceptible to moths unless specially treated.

To hem it all up: pick a design that fits your budget and your lifestyle, and get to hanging, recovering, and draping.

Fabrics intended for home furnishing can be found in any fabric store. Don't be scared to ask salespeople for advice. Most of them are working there because they love to sew, and might even offer to help you with the job, especially if they happen to love Airstreams.

Spark up your creativity and make your Airstream uniquely yours. The great thing about decorating small spaces is that it's generally affordable and even a small change can make a big difference. New curtains or even a new shower curtain can transform the look of the whole trailer.

The interior of an Airstream is often a sun-filled space, which is bad news for some fabrics because they can weaken or fade. So, if you're going to use luxury fabrics in your trailer, make sure you fit blinds or curtains to shade the interior, especially if it's going to sit in the same spot for long periods of time. Fun novelty fabrics can be ordered to reflect your hobbies or to create "trailer chic."

Sometimes a trip to another place might inspire a complete look. If you're traveling and spot a fabric that will help you remember the fun, do like the designers do and tuck a few yards or a bolt in your suitcase. This floral print was picked up in Hawaii and is used here instead of cabinetry—it's lighter and much less expensive.

Some fabrics set the theme. Many designers will tell you to design around one central thing you like. For example, you can use the colors in a bedspread your grandmother made to continue that palette throughout the space.

Kitchenware

Kitchenware is not only practical, it's often also quite beautiful, and the great thing about it is that it is readily available from retro to repro for any style, any taste. Collectors of vintage kitchenware have a cornucopia of items to choose from—from enamelware coffee pots to vintage breadboxes and early iceboxes. And if new is your thing, almost every manufacturer is now carrying reproductions and lines designed especially for small spaces. The important thing to remember when furnishing your Airstream galley kitchen is that it's closet-sized, not residential-sized. Don't buy items that are going to overwhelm the space. And remember to take into consideration electrical requirements. For example, a 220-volt cappuccino maker is probably not a good idea, no matter how good a morning cappuccino would be, if your wiring is 110-volt. When you get a handle on proportions and power, all you have to do is pick what cooks for you.

Shiny or colored, functional or decorative, the kitchen is a place to showcase neat useful things. And unlike other purchases, buying kitchen tools often proves as much fun as using them. By visiting flea markets, estate sales, or early-morning garage sales, you may find some dishes in a harlequin pattern, just like the ones your aunt served ham on every Sunday, or the perfect Depression-glass orange squeezer to make fresh juice on the road. Buyer beware: you may become hopelessly addicted to nifty gadgets… and there's only so much room in your silver box.

One thing to note regarding vintage faucets—sometimes the insides aren't in as good shape as the outside and they often leak or fail to function properly because the years of use can cause washers to lose their seal and the valve seats and stems to break. That's why designers often recommend using reproduction faucets rather than vintage. No, it's not "original," but who needs a leaky faucet when you're supposed to be having fun? There is one caveat from the pros: if it's working okay, don't touch it! Leave well enough alone.

Furniture

Small-space living often requires a few compromises when it comes to decorating, but that doesn't mean it needs to be unattractive. Yes, functionality is the key word in furnishing the interiors of any type of recreational vehicle, but style is also important, as every piece carries weight. All furniture in a small space should do double duty. An attractive sofa or banquette should fold out into a bed; a handy table might be capable of use inside or out, as a desk or for dining.

Designers say that the farther you can see, the larger and more open a space will seem. So when designing inside an Airstream, try to arrange furniture so that it opens up areas of the floor and avoid blocking those windows and all that view.

Scale the furniture to the room, and consider tall furniture rather than wide to preserve valuable floor space. When designing for small spaces, always make sure your furniture can serve two purposes: tables, for example, can serve as a desk or for dining, and ones that completely fold away can be especially useful; benches and any built-in seating should provide hidden room to stash and store. In order to have fun inside your trailer, you'll want to have comfortable, uncluttered surroundings. Make room: furniture, like a good meal, should be savored, not crammed in.

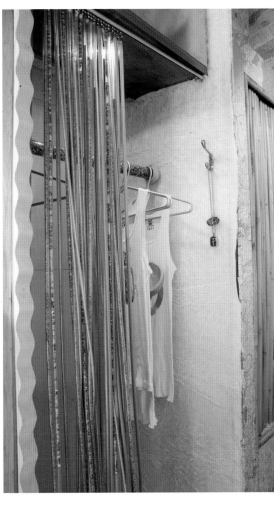

Lighting

Lighting creates ambience and is essential to the look and function of any room. Good lighting makes you feel welcome, highlights colors and objects, and gives a space a sense of life. There are three types of lighting: ambient, task, and accent, and each should serve its purpose without being harsh. Ambient lighting (overhead, hanging, or sconces) casts light uniformly, giving a room a pleasant and livable look. Task lighting (table lamps, swing-arm lamps, or sconces) is focused light that illuminates a specific activity. Accent lights (picture, track, candles) are used to set mood, draw focus, or add sparkle.

Look inside your trailer at different times of the day. How will each area be used? Make sure you take into account the effect of reflective surfaces and how light spills in from the windows.

Before you start to renovate, make a list of what types of lighting you're going to use. If you're using vintage, make sure you rewire. Older wiring is a fire hazard, especially if mice were the last residents.

Bad lighting is a sure way to ruin any mood. So, think it through. There's a myriad of light fixtures available, both old and new. Sconces attach directly to the wall and offer gently filtered and flattering light. The wash that sconces create against a wall adds drama and warmth.

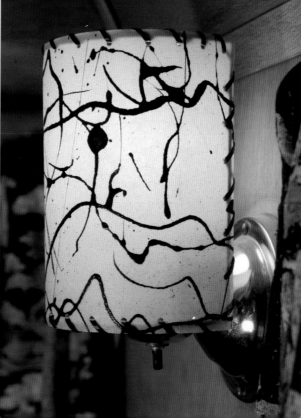

Sconces are a great choice for pale-colored rooms or to complement reflective wall finishes. A wall sconce behind furniture can facilitate reading as well as create a nice ambient glow.

Lamp shades are terrific fashion accessories. Translucent shades, made of natural parchment, paper, linen, or silk, softly diffuse light and create a romantic effect. Opaque shades alter the direction of light and focus the rays up or down.

Bathrooms

When designing a bathroom for a trailer, bigger is not better. Special attention needs to be paid to every detail, because within the confines of a silver shell, there's not the option of removing a closet or breaking down a wall to add space. Finding just the right sink, toilet, or tub could mean the difference between useful and trouble. Small fixtures are comparable in price to, or slightly higher than, regular-sized and are available in home centers and specialty showrooms. Kohler, for example, still makes the small sinks that were originally designed in the 1920s when small sinks were the standard. Can't fit a bathtub? Showers can be custom-made to any dimension, just make sure that the surrounding area isn't water permeable, as splash is always a factor.

Coordination of materials is crucial in small spaces, as everything can be seen at once. Everything has to not only fit, but fit together. Use lighter, cooler colors and reflective surfaces, and tap unused vertical space for storage. Having to use smaller fixtures shouldn't cramp your style and it might even help your budget.

Diminutive sinks and small toilets are readily available, but make sure you can use them efficiently. Wall-hung and corner sinks are great in tight spaces. Just keep in mind that the smaller the sink, the more attention you need to pay to the location and size of the faucet. You don't want to spray the room every time you wash your hands.

Specialty fixtures and fittings are available and often a fun addition. But as you plan your design, be aware of the practicalities. This sink works because it's specifically designed for a makeup and hair trailer. Mosaic tile is stunning in a small space, but if you're traveling with your Airstream, consider the weight it will add.

Details

As they say, "God is in the details." Or is that the Devil? The biggest project depends on the smallest elements to bring it all together. And, in the end, it's usually the smallest things that people notice. Real estate agents report that one of the easiest ways to increase the value of a home, besides a fresh coat of paint and a good clean, is to replace handles and knobs on drawers and cabinets.

The appropriate hardware (cabinet knobs, drawer pulls, door handles, hinges, etc.) can vastly improve the overall impression of your home on wheels. It can transform ordinary doors, cabinets, and furniture into an extraordinary expression of your personal tastes. It's like the perfect icing on a well-risen cake. It makes perfection even sweeter.

The shape and size of handles, knobs, and hinges can be perfectly suited to the time period or theme you've chosen for your trailer design. As you consider the details, note any unusual spacing requirements—the distance between holes, the direction the door opens, the way the old latch is attached. Consider your budget and the overall design of your trailer. Then, make the Internet your friend. Winnow down the literally thousands of choices by putting a description into a search engine and going window shopping.

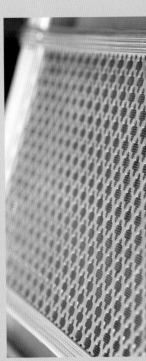

Awnings and Blinds

A relatively economic way to create another room and add value (and excitement and hours of enjoyment) to your trailer is to add an awning. Awnings can be both stylish and functional. Whether you're seeking shelter from the sun or simply jazzing up the backyard, when you add an awning you create an additional outdoor room.

Window coverings and blinds need to fit properly and be sun-resistant. For bright mornings, you may need blackout shades and, if you're taking your show on the road, you'll want to remember that people may park 10 feet away. At 10 feet, they can see nose hairs. The right window coverings can prevent that and make Airstream living much more comfortable.

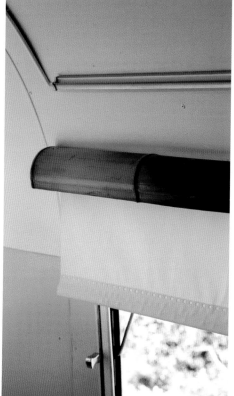

Shades, blinds, and curtains don't have to be expensive, but they do have to fit, especially if you're taking your trailer on the road. To spruce up the ordinary, add attractive finishings. Smoked bamboo for shade caps is an example of a cheap, yet fashionable way to cover the top of inexpensive shades.

An awning not only provides enjoyment, it is also very practical, providing much needed shade for the interior of what can, at times, seem like the inside of a silver convection oven. Many companies will custom-make an awning for your Airstream in a pattern and color of your choosing. Make sure you discuss span—how large an area you want to cover.

Part Five

PRACTICALITIES

How do you get hold of a silver trailer anyway? And once you get one, how do you tow it home? How do you clean it, set it up, and make yours look as good as the ones in this book? These are the questions that every dreamer needs to wake up and answer. Like a first-time mom who has to figure out breastfeeding, diaper changing, and car seats, there are things it's better to know about your baby *before* you bring it home.

The purchase of a silver trailer is exciting, but if you aren't prepared, it can easily turn frustrating and stressful. Do you know where you're going to keep your Airstream? Are there any ordinances in place that might prevent you from keeping it in the spot you have in mind? How are you going to use your trailer? How much renovation is it going to need? Can you afford it? If your dream is to travel cross-country, you'll need to check the axle(s) is in good condition. If not, who is going to repair it? Is your car heavy-duty enough to tow your new purchase?

Thinking things through and preparing in this basic, practical way will make the arrival of your Airstream a dream come true rather than a nightmare. This section is designed to help you think about and understand the essentials of being an owner of rolling real estate, so that you can get it home and *get into it!*

For Sale

I bought my 1963 Silver Streak from a contractor. While he was painting my house he overheard me making calls to people around the country, desperately trying to find an Airstream to use as an outdoor bar for my restaurant, and he casually mentioned his sister was using his as a storage unit. For $400 she found another place to put her Christmas ornaments and folding patio chairs, and I realized my silver dream.

My friend Aidan Quinn and his wife Elizabeth walked up to a house that had an Airstream in the driveway, knocked on the door, and asked if it was for sale. Next thing you know they were towing it into their backyard. But what do you do if you're not lucky enough to have a contractor who has one or movie-star blue eyes that can convince anyone to sell you anything?

You hunt for vintage or you buy new. Airstream, Inc., is still rolling them off the line—manufacturing over 2,500 trailers a year—with models ranging from the sporty Nissan Base Camp at around $20,000 to the ultimate, top-of-the-line 39-foot SkyDeck, complete with rooftop terrace, spiral staircase, and a $250,000 price tag.

Or rather than buy new, you may decide to head back to the future and roll into vintage. Sixty percent of all Airstreams ever made are estimated to still be in service, although finding a vintage model that's

Buyer beware: used trailers may have structural flaws that aren't evident without an inspection. Check for rear-end sag (when the frame is bent because of improper interior balance), and for worn out axles, which is a serious safety issue that can result in collapse. Both problems are fixable, just at a price.

in good shape paired with an owner who's willing to part with it is another story, and those are being snapped up faster than you can say retro.

Airstream president Dicky Riegel bought a rare 1954 Flying Cloud Custom from a lady in western Pennsylvania who had owned it since new. "It was a backyard find," he says gleefully. "It had been sitting in her woods for 26 years and she was using it for storage. She wanted to give it to me for free because she knew it would have a good home." Dicky purchased it (he insisted on paying), called on his connections to get it renovated, and now it's living large at Airstream headquarters in Ohio, towed by a 1954 Chevy truck. Incidentally, what does the president of Airstream suggest: vintage or new? "Get one of each," he says quickly. After all, he did. Besides the Flying Cloud, he has a 2005 16-foot Bambi Quiksilver, which he uses as a pool house.

Don't fret. You don't have to be the president of Airstream to realize your silver dream. There *are* ways to find them: scour websites, classifieds, and generally keep your eyes peeled. You never know when you'll spot one tied up in a backyard like a lonely dog. If there's not a "Beware of Airstream" sign outside, don't be afraid to knock on the door and say you admire it.

But finding one is only the beginning of the adventure…

Take Care

Perhaps you were so excited when you saw the love of your life with the bargain basement "for sale" sign in the window that you failed to notice she had a few flaws. Or perhaps you noticed every single one, but looked past them. Either way, there are some telltale signs to be aware of, because they may point to bigger problems lurking beneath the silvery outer skin.

A soft spot in the floor or wall, for example, may be something more than a surface blemish. That soft spot may indicate extensive rot—and the ramifications of this may be the necessary removal of a section of the floor or wall, or the entire floor or wall, in order to make the interior once again structurally safe.

Virtually all of us have mold somewhere in our home, but if a lot of mold exists, it's not a healthy environment. Moldy walls or curtains may be relatively harmless, but "black mold" (a slimy, greenish-black mold) is a serious health risk. You can use a mixture of one cup bleach to a gallon of water to disinfect the area, but be aware that spores from dried mold are dangerous and should be cleaned with caution. If the area is infested (over 2 square feet), consult a professional.

Mouse poop or stashed nuts in the toilet or kitchen cabinets are obvious indicators of another resident in your silver palace, and unfortunately, even if he's checked out, he might have left behind a wiring nightmare. Rodents will chew through any wires in their path, which can lead to a circuitry breakdown or, worse, a fire. If you see evidence of chewed wires, you may want an electrician to inspect the damage and, if necessary, do a rewire.

Some trailers, particularly those with rear baths, develop rear-end sag, whereby the trailer frame becomes bent, cracked, or separated. A quick test is to step on the bumper and push down. If there's any separation between the frame and the body, you may be looking at a serious, potentially expensive structural problem.

Like repainting a dull room is a quick interior design fix, one of the greatest improvements for an Airstream is a good polish. It's exhausting, but worth it.

Keeping debris off the top of a parked trailer will help prevent tarnishing, but take precautions before climbing on top. A good ladder is a good investment.

The best advice is to take time to examine a trailer in detail, so you'll know what it's going to require to make it roadworthy or to bring it up to your standards. This isn't to say a trailer with any one or all of these problems wouldn't be worth the effort—just know that you may have to deal with a few annoyances, both financial and physical, in order to make your home away from home sweet.

HIGH PRO GLOW

Like us, as trailers age their skin tends to lose its youthful luster, but a glowing trailer is what we all want and it's the surefire way to stop the neighbors whispering "yard refuse" and start admiring your "classic." Though polishing is an arduous task, it's possible to bring even the dullest aluminum back to its original mirror finish, and there are a number of "how to" sites on the Internet (some of which are listed in the Tour Guide on page 156). Here are some top tips:

- Buy yourself a quality electric buffer/polisher, like a Rolite Aircraft Polisher or Cyclo 5 Dual Head.
- Use a proven metal polish like Nuvite or Rolite, available in specialty hardware stores or online.
- Set yourself up with scaffolding. This can be two A-frame ladders with a plank between the two, or genuine scaffolding from a local equipment rental company.
- Invest in a lot of 100 percent cotton rags (no polyester stitching). Old sweatshirt material works great.
- Put your trailer in a spot that you're not scared to see covered in black, and wear clothes you're not scared to see covered in black.
- Start with coarser polish for the first run, finishing with finest for the last buff. At each step—you'll need to go over it at least three times—remove all trace of black oxidation. You won't believe the black, but you'll be happy with the finish!

Getting Hitched

When I was around 11 years old, my dad borrowed a friend's trailer so he could take my brother and me camping. As we arrived at our campsite, he asked me to get out of the car and help guide him in between two trees. "You got it! You got it!" I encouraged, waving him in like the best airport ground crew. CRUNCH. I'll never forget the sound and I'll never forget my dad's face when he got out of the car and saw the damage. "I didn't want to *get* it!" he steamed. "I wanted to *miss* it!" We never went camping again.

When the time comes to take your trailer on the road, make sure that you are prepared. Consider the following tips, a quick crash course, to prevent, well, crashing:

First off, check whether your tow vehicle has the capacity to tow the weight of your trailer. If so, check your tow vehicle's hitch. Make this and other preventive checks—on wheel bearings, tire pressure, suspension, and lights, for example—part of your packing routine each and every time you plan to hit the road.

Perhaps the most confusing part of driving a trailer is backing up. It's almost like reverse steering. Follow the advice of my truck driver friend and change the position of your hands on the steering wheel. Rather than placing your hands at 11 o'clock and 2 o'clock, place them both on the bottom of the wheel. The direction you turn the wheel is the direction your trailer will turn. It sounds nutty, but it works.

The greatest wheels and tires in the world will do no good if the suspension isn't up to hauling all that weight. Have someone help you check your lights. With you in the tow car and someone watching the backend of your trailer, check your brake lights and turn signals. If they aren't in proper working order, it is an obvious danger to both you and others on the road.

Pack It Up

All the fun and convenience of a home away from home hits the skids if you forget to take the things you need. My neighbor, Mr. Simmons, always had his wife check off a list as they packed their Airstream each weekend for the lake. His preprinted list covered everything from folding and stowing the lawn chairs to pinning the refrigerator door.

The Airstream is probably one of the most space-efficient vehicles ever made. It had to be. Remember, if she was going camping, Wally's wife wanted all the conveniences of home. Inside an Airstream, there are storage compartments and bins everywhere you look. Utilize them wisely. Store wet or soiled items in the rear bumper storage and exterior compartments designed to house hoses, and wrap breakables such as picture frames and souvenirs in clothes before stowing them in the under-bed storage drawers or bins.

What would Wally do? Wherever he was headed, he was always prepared. He knew where he'd be filling up for gas, where to get water, and how much food to stock. As well as the typical staples (like salt, toilet paper, and coffee filters) make sure you carry an extra water hose, as well as a jack, tool set, duct tape, and basic spare parts. Some of the places you find yourself journeying to could be quite remote.

See You On the Road

Few things capture the fun and American spirit more than the story that is Airstream. The joy of these space-age capsules, as you've seen, is that they can take on any personality, any style, and can be used for adventures both near and far. Whether you're an owner or just a dreamer, the shiny aluminum pod that Wally made is a legend in any time, and as my friend actress Frances McDormand told me, "It's not something you need, it's something you just have to have."

I've had great delight in meeting those inimitable people who revere these uniquities and seeing the results of their creative minds. I'm smitten with both them and their silver beauties. But now, as with every story, every trip, it's time to turn the page and move on to a new adventure. As Wally said, we don't say "goodbye," we say, "See you on the road…"

Until then, may all your silver dreams come true…

Tour Guide

Here are a few sites to see…

airstream.com—this is the official site of Airstream where you can explore the future, delve into historical archives, connect with other Airstreamers, find a dealer, and get the latest Airstream buzz.

airstream-bohemia.com—amazing resource for vintage Airstream restorers. The site offers advice, catalogs silver trailer press clips, great links, and has a database in which you can find your model or register your serial number.

airstreamcentral.com—ask questions, get answers. They won't make fun of you, even when you ask the most elementary of questions. Trust me.

airstreamdreams.com—hard-to-get parts, supplies, and fun merchandise for Airstreams and other vintage travel trailers and motor homes.

airstreameurope.com—the first Airstream campsite in Europe. Also provides information and repairs.

airstreamforums.com—informative discussions run the gamut from where to find one to how to fix a leaky water tank.

airstreamlife.com—the only official Airstream-specific lifestyle magazine. Subscribe! It's terrific fun.

birchwoodbeauties.com—a terrific vintage travel trailer restoration company in northern California. They offer a nice collection of vintage trailers for purchase and lots of good ideas.

careyhultgren.com—designer's site offers everything from consultation to entire trailer interior design.

coolknobsandpulls.com—a great source for cabinet hardware at discount prices. Unique and distinctive hardware for kitchen, baths, and furniture.

ebay.com—hundreds of Airstream-related items, from belt buckles to the real deal.

eurostream.co.uk—your place on the web if you're in Europe and want to find out how to get an Airstream.

hardwaresource.com—an inventory of over 25,000 hinges for every kind of door and cabinet imaginable.

jpadrapes.com—replacement draperies for your silver trailer with sunlight-resistant lining. Thirty years' experience of making drapes for Airstream and Argosy. Free fabric samples.

myknobs.com—a spot where designers turn for the right hardware. They offer over 120,000 knobs, handles, and pulls to choose from.

oldhousejournal.com—tons of great renovation ideas featuring inspiration, ideas, and resources to re-create yesterday for today's living.

perfectpolish.com—site offering the materials and techniques necessary to bring bare aluminum surfaces to a mirrorlike finish.

recreationalvehiclesecrets.com—a wide variety of links and information on recreational vehicles, motor homes, and trailers with new articles and resources updated daily. Sign up for the RV information newsletter.

rvdumps.com—tells you where in each state you can unload or fill your tanks and offers interesting facts like, "Louisiana becomes nation's first 'RV Friendly' state."

silvertrailer.com—art, design, and neat things around the airstream theme.

skyriverrv.com—offers everything you need for your Airstream, including a full service department and a complete parts and accessories center.

tincantourists.com—an organization committed to the celebration of classic trailers and motor coaches through annual gatherings of owners and friends! Subscribe for free and receive classified ads for trailers, parts, questions, and advice.

trailertrashé.com—your source for trailer chic. They scour trailer parks, flea markets, and dime stores around America to find the most stylish, glamorous, and functional accessories to complement your trailer.

vintageairstream.com—there is no "bluebook" for Airstreams, but this website is an excellent resource for determining fair market value, providing photos of vintage Airstreams listed by year and length. Amazing resource!

vintagetrailering.com—restorations, renovations, and modernizations. Anything you can imagine, they can design and build. Creator of the "Home Sweet Home" screen door guard.

vintagevacations.com—a full-service shop that produces the finest restorations and renovations available on all types of vintage and classic travel trailers and motor homes. The site is filled with information on many of the several thousand trailers' names and models that have been built.

wbcci.org—the oldest RV association in the world. Includes information on caravans, rallies, membership, history, maintenance, classifieds, and a forum.

Index

Acknowledgments

A ROUND OF APPLAUSE

What a joy it has been talking to all these wonderful people about something so downright fun. A heartfelt thanks to all those who let us step into their "home away from home" and snoop around. Traveling the countryside with photographer and new friend Simon Brown was a delight, even when we were fending off snarling junkyard dogs to get the perfect picture of a silver beauty. We had a lot of laughs and both of us hope our passion shows. Thanks to Liz, Lois, Milo, and Finn who Simon missed so much while he was Stateside shooting.

Big thanks to Peter Bridgewater, Sophie Collins, and all at Ivy Press. Judith More you're so clever, and Anna Davies, what a hunter! Caroline Earle thank you for your organization, thoroughness, and your uncanny ability to get English charm into every email! And to design geniuses Karl Shanahan and Bernard Higton—wow! At HarperCollins, this book received the royal treatment from Harriet Pierce, Ilana Anger, and publicity mastermind Gretchen Crary.

Thanks, too, to Airstream and its President Dicky Riegel and Director of Marketing Tim Champ, who came through with everything we needed. And to Laura and Wesley Barchenger, Birchwood Beauties, Fenwick Bonnell, Lee Clower, Christopher Deam, Chris Dow, Johnnie Dymock, Global Icons, Carey Hultgren, Adrian Kahan, Clare Kelly and David Barra, Alexia Kondylis, Ralph Lauren, Atelier Van Lieshout, the Marcinik Family, Nina Marinkovich, Vince Martinico, Tim Pfeiffer, Aidan and Elizabeth Quinn, Jason Reed, Cynthia Rowley, Kristiana Spaulding, Andrea and Alan Spaulding, Anne-Katrin Spiess, Paul Welschmeyer, and Laura Woodroffe, for sharing their silver dreams.

Extraordinary gratitude and love to Scott Stewart, my partner and friend, who is always up for a new adventure, and to Chef Jonathan Sheridan and our restaurant teams at the Rosendale Cement Company and The Alamo for always keeping things cookin' while I'm off writing. And Cenaida Johannes for keeping our house a home, while I'm home writing. And my agent Todd Shuster at Zachary Shuster Harmsworth for keeping me writing. Big credit goes to artist Greg Arnett and contractor Dave Wyncoop who helped me create the interior of the "World's Only Silver Streak Bar" and Mary Cleary who made the garden for it to live in. To Stephan Jablonski, who came to paint the house and is still creating masterpieces, I say I will always believe in you.

Lastly, during the course of writing this book, two important friends died: Our dear dog Jasper—my writing partner and loyal companion—who taught me to find joy in the everyday and without whom we would have never found a place in the country; and Harry Skerritt, affable contractor and building inspector, who sold me his Silver Streak (page 112) and made my silver dreams come true. May their heavenly clouds have a silver lining.

And to you for believing that something special is always over the next hill…

See you on the road!

Bruce

PICTURE CREDITS

The publisher would like to thank the following organizations and individuals for their kind permission to reproduce the photographs in this book. Every effort has been made to acknowledge the pictures, however we apologize if there are any unintentional omissions.

Atelier Van Lieshout (Bais-o-drome): 93, 96–97
Lee Clower: 130–131
Chris Dow: 54 bottom, 55 top and bottom left
Johnnie Dymock: 120–121
Bill Hatcher: 106–109
Bill Geddes (Alexia Kondylis/design): 98–101, 141 top
Global Icons: 6, 8, 9–10, 16–17, 18–19, 20–21 (except top left), 22–23, 24–25, 135 bottom left, 142 right, 154, 154–155 center, 156
Mark J. Marcinik: 135 top left
Neil Michel/Axiom: 126–127, 134 right
Michael O'Callahan: 56–57, 140
Paul Welschmeyer: 54 top, 55 bottom right
Ted Yarwood: 94–95

All other photographs taken by Simon Brown.